God Was Not Silent
The Case for the Forgotten Books

Father Michael Pacella III
John W. Stanko

urbanpress

God Was Not Silent

by Father Michael Pacella III & John W. Stanko

Copyright ©2023 Father Michael Pacella III & John W. Stanko

ISBN 978-1-63360-209-0

For Worldwide Distribution
Printed in the U.S.A.

Urban Press
P.O. Box 8881
Pittsburgh, PA 15221-0881
412.646.2780

Chapter 1 - The Sacred Books

Chapter 2 - The Book of Tobit

Chapter 3 - The Book of Judith

Chapter 4 - First and Second Maccabees

Chapter 5 - Esther With the Greek Extension

PREFACE

Father Michael Pacella and I have been friends for 40 years. We have laughed, cried, talked, prayed, and learned together and that learning took us at one point on separate paths. Father Michael and I were both pastors, dare I say evangelical pastors, when we each decided we needed more theological education than we had. Father Michael went on to Yale and Harvard and then Cambridge University, all academic heavyweights, while I went on to Liberty Theological and Reformed Presbyterian Seminary, not quite in the same league or tradition.

Then he re-entered the military and I went in and out of church work, eventually founding a nonprofit organization and also starting a publishing company which led me to spend a lot of time in Africa. We always kept in touch, however, and I followed Father Michael's journey through the military and into his appreciation and call to a more liturgical approach to worship, which combined his deep love for learning and appreciation for the historical doctrines of the church. I could not keep up with his brilliance or zeal for knowledge, but I did my best to encourage him in his endeavors to find and fulfill his purpose, which included his academic pursuits as well as priestly ministry.

After Father Michael's daughter tragically passed away in 2016, I encouraged him to take his seminar material on ethics he had been presenting to law enforcement and military personnel and put it into a book. I was honored that he chose my publishing company, Urban Press, to publish his outstanding work. I have to admit that when he first told me about his seminar and that he taught it in full clerical garb, complete with white collar, I thought, "Now how relevant is that going to be? How well will his audience relate to him and his presentation? It's probably over their heads!" That just shows my bias and ignorance of Father Michael's call and his God-given ability to translate what could be dry and academic material into something relevant and meaningful for men and women in uniform. By the way, let me include a shameless plug for that outstanding book titled *From Valor to Virtue: The Moral Development of the Brave*, available on Amazon in paper and Kindle formats.

Therefore, when we started talking about collaborating on a book that focused on the Apocrypha, I had learned my lesson and was careful not to dismiss it as irrelevant or not that interesting. In fact, I had never read the Apocryphal books, so it presented something of a challenge to me to continue my learning and expand my horizons. And let me say here that I will refer to these books as *Apocryphal* or the *Apocrypha* throughout this book while Father Michael will use the more Catholic term *Deuterocanonical*. We will do that because while Father Michael became a part of the Charismatic Episcopal Church, I remained an evangelical pastor working out of my local church that is part of the Christian and Missionary Alliance denomination.

While we serve the Lord in two separate streams, make no mistake that Father Michael and I share a love for the Lord, His word, His Church, and His people. When we get together, we still laugh, cry, pray, talk, and share life lessons as well as brag about our grandchildren and wives, who are both creative and talented women. But I digress, for I was describing our decision to write the book you hold in your hand.

When Father Michael proposed this book, I had just begun teaching a class named "The Gospels "at Ottawa University in Kansas, not Canada. I had been doing extensive reading and research on the period of time leading up to Jesus' birth and of course kept "bumping into" references to books like First and Second Maccabees. I wanted to distill what I was learning into a concise introduction for the Gospels course, but there was no way to fit it into the short, eight-week semester or term that Ottawa uses. Therefore, I produced an introductory video that explained the world for a few centuries prior to Jesus' birth and made it an extra-credit assignment for the students.

Thus, when Father Michael proposed we study and write about the Apocrypha, I was all in because I knew it would give me a better understanding of the Jewish audience to whom Jesus spoke. I would then better understand what shaped their worldview and why so many of them had such a difficult time grasping Jesus' message. Of course, this meant I had to read the Apocrypha, which I did. I found it to be tedious at times, but fascinating and enlightening on other occasions.

Now you may ask, "Why would you or why would I want to read something that is tedious at times?" I would answer for the same reasons we read Numbers, or Leviticus, or First Chronicles. Parts of those books are not as gripping as the narratives in historical books, but they are valuable. In fact, we often skip those parts that are "tedious" or boring to get to the "good stuff." The same holds true for Judith, Ecclesiasticus, Sirach, and the other books of the Apocrypha. They require some mining to get to the gold, which when found, makes it all the more valuable.

The Apocryphal books helped shape the mindset and worship experience for Jesus' contemporaries and, as you will read in my later chapters, were the main reason they misinterpreted His message that the Kingdom had come. They were conditioned by thinking for 400 years prior to His coming that soon it would be their turn to rule the world and they couldn't wait. Jesus came along and said, "My Kingdom is not of this world," and many of His listeners responded, "Sorry, that can't be God. I'm out of here."

You may want to read the Apocryphal books before you start reading this book. Better yet, we suggest that you give us 28 days and read parts of them along with us as we describe their relevance for you in the devotional that follows. Sometimes knowing what you are looking for or its value helps your reading comprehension. Therefore, we have prepared 28 devotionals complete with questions to help you apply and reflect on what you have read (Father Michael wrote them and I did the editing and added the questions). Once you see the value in the Apocryphal books and how they fit into the New Testament message, perhaps they will be easier to engage and read. I know I am the better equipped for reading them and have used many quotes from them in my other writings. I'm confident you will do the same.

My thanks to Father Michael who tolerated my questions and perspectives that I know were far removed from and below his knowledge and understanding. He has patiently shepherded me through this project and I have learned much from what he has written in conjunction with our discussions. This book also gave me a good excuse to visit him in the wonderful city of Williamsburg, Virginia, where he lives with his delightful wife, Doreen.

You will read more of what I have to say throughout the book, for my main emphasis, as I already stated, is to see what we can learn from the Apocrypha to help us understand how first-century Jews interpreted and misinterpreted Jesus' message. You will not be surprised to discover that their reasons for missing His meaning still apply today to modern readers who also grapple with understanding what Jesus really said in the politically-charged culture in which we live.

Dr. John W. Stanko
Pittsburgh, PA
February 2023

INTRODUCTION AND BACKGROUND

My thanks to my friend and colleague, Dr. John Stanko, for his kind words in his preface. We have been friends for many years, which has made this project all the more special for me. Not only do I have the chance to write about something about which I am passionate, but I also get to do it with a friend and brother. John's perspective and input into this book are important, for his various trips to Israel and his experience as a university professor have all enriched my own studies and application of what I have learned. We have a mutual admiration for one another's calling and ministry, and I'm sure that will come through loud and clear as you read.

Let me start by giving you some background for what you are about to read as John has already done. There was an earnest debate in the first four centuries of the early church about which books to accept and include in the sacred canon of Scripture. Saint Augustine, then the bishop of Hippo, played a major role in leading the discussion and ensuring that the early councils discussing this matter were held in Africa. Augustine was the first major figure in the Church to set forth a list of biblical books, which included all the disputed Old Testament books without making any distinction between the fully canonical Hebrew books and the lesser books derived from the Septuagint (don't worry, we will define words like *canon* and *Septuagint* later).

The books that were admitted from the canon of the Septuagint have always been revered by church historians and bishops alike. St. Augustine provided the best explanation for the acceptance of these books into the canon of Scripture by providing a detailed explanation of each book while also sharing why each should be considered a part of sacred Scripture.

Once the list of books was determined, he sent it to Rome for ratification. There were five Sees at that time, with Rome being the first among equals. It was declared that 72 or 73 books were the only ones that could be read in church because some were already accustomed to reading works like the *Shepherd of Hermas*, considering it to be Scripture. This and others like it were good works, but the bishops came together by the Holy Spirit and decided that only those 72 were the ones that had the seal of the Holy Spirit as inspired.

We believe Paul was writing God's inspired Word when he wrote Philippians or any of his epistles for that matter. Centuries later, the bishops came together and determined that the Deuterocanonical books were the equal of Paul's writings. When Peter talked about Paul's writings, he pointed out that untaught people distorted them as they do the "rest of the scriptures" and in Peter's mind, he was referring to the Old Testament Hebrew canon, which included what we have come to consider the "extra books."

There's much documentation and authority from the Ecumenical Councils to insinuate that these books are anything but sacred. For example, it's interesting that Jesus referred to the book of Jonah on more than a few occasions. Some liberal theologians dismiss the book with his name as a myth. However, Jesus said we must heed Scripture so if He quoted and believed in the story of Jonah, then we should as well. In my mind that includes the books that Jesus would have been familiar with.

When I teach Old Testament classes at a Catholic university, I have the freedom to teach from all the genre known as the Wisdom Literature. God knows how badly we need wisdom in our day, so I think we should be open to finding it in any godly source. We have Proverbs and Ecclesiastes, but there's a lot more wisdom to be found in *Ecclesiasticus* or *Sirach*, and the *Wisdom of Solomon*. We also have the elaborations from the Greek writings of Daniel and Esther. There are some important, significant things to be found there.

Judith

I also appreciate the wisdom in a book like *Judith*, which I happen to love. The reader has to understand the genre and what the Lord was trying to express through it. Some evangelicals try to make Genesis a science book, which it was not intended to be. Often people don't understand the genre of something like apocalyptic literature. Readers often want to interpret it literally but that is not correct or wise.

Dr. Stanko mentioned in the preface that I've taught military personnel and law enforcement officers about morality and ethics. I have drawn some of my material from all the wisdom books, not just Proverbs or Ecclesiastes. There's so much there that we can't afford to miss. As another example of practical wisdom that is relevant for today, I focused on Ecclesiasticus 38 during the pandemic because it teaches us that God is the ultimate healer, but He often uses physicians and pharmacists to do His work. I hope you get my point that there is much in these neglected books that we can use and need in the twenty-first century.

Judith, the main character in the book with

her name, is a worthwhile example of men and women who are called to take the great risks for God. She is part of the company of women God has used throughout history to accomplish His will, women like Deborah in the book of Judges; Mary, the mother of Jesus; Elizabeth, the mother of John the Baptist; and many other women who assisted and led ministry outreaches during the time of the apostles.

God did not call these women to be priests or prophets, but they wielded extraordinary power and influence among the people. In Genesis 3:15, the Lord said, "I will put enmity between you and the woman between your offspring and her offspring. She will crush your head and you will lie in wait for her heel." This is consistent with the account of Judith beheading Holofernes as reported in Judith 13:8. The New Testament teaches that there is neither male nor female in Christ, which means that God wants to use everyone in their sphere of competency.

It doesn't matter what title you have or the position you hold. Male or female, you can be an influencer and that is what both *Esther* and *Judith* teach us. They weren't ordained or the titular head of anything. These women proved that they did not have to be the head to make a difference, just like Joseph, who was the second in command and had more influence than the Pharaoh himself. The most important person God used in a significant way is the Virgin Mary, who we call Theotokos, or the God-bearer. The church cannot be biased against women in ministry for there's no one who is more highly esteemed by God than Mary, the mother of Jesus.

Muslims and many other groups have a high regard for Mary, except for evangelicals, who usually only give Mary attention around Christmas time. There's always been a high regard even for her mother, Saint Anne, with a few feast days recognizing her significance. The organization with which I now identify doesn't ordain women and we certainly don't see examples of any priestesses in the Old Testament. We do, however, see women prophets and women servers in the New Testament.

Catholic Bias?

Let me pause here and talk a bit about why I believe there has been such bias against the Deuterocanonical books. Today it is estimated that there are 40,000 denominations. Of course, before the Reformation, that was not the case—there was one church. I don't think it was Luther's intent to divide the body of Christ; there was no way he could have imagined what we have today in the way of sects, church groups, and governing bodies. Martin Luther restored some important things to the Church that had been lost over the centuries. Pope John Paul II went to a Lutheran church in Rome to celebrate his memory on Luther's 500th birthday and recognize him for his emphasis on the priesthood of believers and justification by faith.

Yet after the Reformation, there was a tendency to reject something just because it was connected with Rome and the Catholic Church. In regards to some things, we threw out the baby with the bath water. In some matters, we rejected the wisdom of the church fathers. St. Thomas Aquinas is one of my heroes. I can't read his material without coming across references to these Deuterocanonical works. So, how do we handle that? Do we reject all he wrote because he was Catholic? What do we lose if and when we do that? We have the oral tradition of the Church, and it's important that we adhere to it—or at least heed what it was trying to say: "So then, brothers and sisters, stand firm and hold on to the traditions which you were taught, whether by word of mouth or by letter from us" (2 Thessalonians 2:15, NASB).

It's not the traditions of men but traditions we call holy or sacred tradition. Those are practices that were passed down. Jesus addressed the traditions of men that invalidated the word of God. I know the difference, but we have a great heritage. You have got to understand if we didn't have the Bible, the way we have known it now for 400 years, how would the Church exist? We had bishops, priests, deacons. If you look at the earliest record of the Sunday service, it's very close to what you see in the Mass. There are prayers and readings. We see the Eucharist, which is central. This was from Justin the Martyr who was sharing with the political powers of his day what Christians did. It's vital that we understand the importance of this whole corpus of information when we begin talking about the Septuagint which was created around 250 BC.

I sat under Brevard Childs as an Old Testament professor at Yale. He's one of the top ten Old Testament theologians in the world. I thank God for training from somebody like him. He taught that when we look at the New Testament quotes from the Old Testament, they are from the Septuagint. That's why sometimes we find some inconsistencies among what we read in the Old and what is quoted in the New. Therefore, we shouldn't dismiss the Septuagint and say it wasn't the Bible that Paul and Jesus used because it was. We must be careful not to formulate doctrine from the Deuterocanonical books alone, but what I'm trying to appeal to is the fact that they substantiate what's already there.

The people of God should acknowledge and learn from the moving historical accounts found in *First and Second Maccabees*. We should admire and seek to emulate their heroic examples of commitment and dedication as people who stood for God in the face of death. Hanukkah commemorates the rededication of the temple in 165 BC by the Maccabees after its desecration by the Syrians as described in those two books. It is celebrated by Jews to this day.

This miraculous intervention refutes the concept that God was not speaking or acting in the four centuries between Malachi in the Old Testament and the gospel of Matthew in the New. The sacrifice and torture that our forebearers endured should encourage us to be bold in our generation regarding our witness, testimony, and our service.

I refer especially to *Second Maccabees* 7:41, where it states, "Then last of all, after the sons, the mother also was consumed." The whole family gave their lives in the hope of a future resurrection spurred on by their noble mother, who also sacrificed her life for the truth of God's word. These heroes, and God knows we need heroes in today's world, are the best examples we have in Hebrew history of true death-defying courage, along with many outstanding stories in the *Book of Daniel* along with its Greek extensions, to be explained in a future devotion.

Esther

Esther is an important book in the corpus of Holy Writ, yet many maintain that the name of God is missing from the book and therefore should not be included in the Canon of Scripture. However, the Greek version extension mentions God 50 times, making this so-called secular or non-God book a God-centered one. Mordecai and Esther were God-fearing people who obeyed God's law and engaged in holy practices like fasting and prayer.

Therefore, it would not be logical to think that they did not have or operate from a Hebrew or a godly perspective. This book cannot be properly understood without the godly worldview that only the extended Greek version provides.

Esther and Mordecai had a worldview that included God's willingness to intervene in history and protect His people. Do you have a worldview that includes God, and that describes the problem in the world and the remedy for it through Christ? Do you live this worldview? Can you explain and defend it? Like Esther, you were born for such a time as this. Do you know your purpose? Are you facing a dilemma in your life or work, and if so, perhaps it's time to pray and fast like Esther, Mordecai, and other Jews did.

Daniel and the Greek Extension

Daniel and *the Greek Extension* also present an interesting contrast to what we have in Daniel without that extension. The first chapter of the Greek extension relates the story of Susanna who was accused by two elders of being unfaithful to her husband through an adulterous affair in her garden, supposedly observed by the accusing elders.

She's speedily convicted because of the position and status of her accusers and was condemned to death. Daniel appeared on the scene and astutely questioned the elders separately as to under which tree the affair took place. They both gave different answers, and were found to be lying because of their own lust and desire for Susanna. They even insisted that during the trial, her face remain uncovered so they could behold her beauty. It was then that the people realized Daniel had the gift of prophecy and discernment, and he was invited to sit among the elders of God's people.

I recommend that you read the inspiring story and see God's justice firsthand being delivered by a young man with a prophetic gift. That's where he was first recognized as a prophet. That title or role didn't come down from heaven; it was bestowed on him by people who saw his gift function.

Based on your re-reading of Daniel, let me ask you some questions to help you apply what you have learned (which is what I will also do in the next section after each of the devotionals). Do you know your spiritual gifts? Do you recognize those around you who have the ability to hear from God and communicate what they hear? Who are they? Do you have such a gift? Are you quick to jump to conclusions before hearing all sides of the story? Can you think of a time when you did not? What were the circumstances of this? What were the circumstances or results of this rush to judgment? Do you see the abundant spiritual lessons available from reading just the first few chapters of Daniel's Greek extension?

Baruch

Baruch was Jeremiah's scribe. Jeremiah is said to have left behind a letter, clarifying the works of God as he observed them during the days of the prophet Jeremiah. Baruch's letter is especially important for it provides more context to better understand the ministry challenges, content, and context of Jeremiah.

Another example of this is Luke and his relationship to Paul, which enabled Luke to provide valuable context and insight into the work of Paul at the time he was in ministry. Luke probably did his research for and writing of both his gospel and Acts while Paul was in prison in Caesarea, staying close to Paul in Jerusalem for those years.

History tells us that the apostle Peter was the source for John Mark when he wrote the gospel of Mark. St. Prochorus is said to have been the scribe for John, the theologian, as he is referred to in church history. All these relationships are significant, which is the reason of Baruch's letter is so significant for us today.

Wisdom of Solomon

The *Wisdom of Solomon* complements the material found in the Wisdom Literature of the Old Testament, or as some prefer to call it the First Testament. The current moral state of the world and the Church necessitates that we not ignore any of God's wisdom, wherever it is found, which makes all the wisdom books important. This is God's truth. We need wisdom, not only in the form of rules, but also in how and where to apply true knowledge as we learn and digest it. The sages of Jewish history have left us nuggets of wisdom in a practical framework, including books like the Wisdom of Solomon.

There are no shortcuts to wisdom and knowledge. The Holy Spirit can't do the work that only each believer can do. That includes study, application, reflection, correction, and feedback. The Scriptures teach that we should not move the ancient boundaries (see Proverbs 22:28) but instead should adhere to the parameters established by God and all His word and historical documents and precedents of the Church to make sure we never cross the line where biblical truth is concerned. First, what can you do to grow in wisdom and knowledge? Do you have a plan? Second, what are you doing to increase your understanding of biblical and church history? Third, if you are wise, what do you do to make that wisdom available for the good of others?

An example I use with my students is that we are required to read the driver's manual where it talks about hydro-planing so we pass the book test. Then we get in a car and have to apply what we read by slowing down when it rains or by not braking too fast. That's applied knowledge or wisdom. We talk about loving wisdom, so therefore we need to read and absorb as much wisdom as possible from as many sources as possible. Then we need to apply it. That's the reason I think the Deuterocanonical Wisdom Literature is important but neglected literature. I regularly taught out of this material when I was in the military.

In searching the Scriptures, I find 400 Old Testament references in the book of Revelation. My point is that the New Testament is full of Old Testament references, including mentions of images or concepts from the Deuterocanonical books. Consider these instances from the Gospels.

- Matthew 2:16: Herod's decree of slaying the innocent children was prophesied in Wisdom 11:7.

- Matthew 7:16-20: Jesus' statement that you will know them by their fruits follows Sirach 27:6. The fruit discloses the cultivation.

- Matthew 9:36: The people were like sheep without a shepherd is the same as in Judith 11:19.

- Matthew 22:25; Mark 12:20; Luke 20:29: The gospel writers could be referring to the canonicity of Tobit 3:8 and 7:11 regarding the seven brothers.

- John 5:18: Jesus claiming that God is His father follows Wisdom 2:16.

- Luke 21:24: Jesus' usage of falling by the edge of the sword follows Sirach 28:18.

It would make sense that since these books were part of the Septuagint, Jesus would have been familiar with them. Then He would naturally draw from them in His public ministry and teaching. If those books were part of our Lord's repertoire of resources, then they should be part of ours.

In the school where my wife is an administrator, I can't teach third grade science because I don't have a science degree and am not certified while every teacher in that school can teach Bible without any biblical training. Yet James wrote that not many of us should be teachers because we will incur a stricter judgment. We should take that admonition seriously. We should study to show ourselves a workman who needs not be ashamed, rightly dividing the word of truth. It's not a suggestion, it's a command.

The *Wisdom of Solomon* may very well have come from the Solomonic tradition, for I am sure there was much of Solomon's wisdom circulating in the world many years after his departure. Wisdom is a fascinating concept, but hard to find. When God gifts a man or a woman with wisdom, it is a major blessing to their lives and they in turn make it a blessing in the lives of others.

None of our gifts are ever for simply personal consumption. The queen of Sheba commented that God's love was exhibited by the good and wise leader God provided His people by giving them a great leader like King Solomon. What does that tell us concerning how God feels about us today, because He doesn't always give us good leaders?

The wisdom literature in Holy Scripture is a gift from God. The Proverbs of Solomon are a godsend as are the other books that fall into the wisdom category. Practical advice and ethical parameters are provided to aid a well-lived life. There is often good advice about friendships.

As I've said many times in conversation, common sense is not that common. This is the very reason we must be trained by the wisdom literature of the Bible, which exhorts us to heed the voices of our parents and other significant people God has placed in our lives.

Bel and the Dragon is an intriguing and interesting account of the wisdom of God working through the prophet Daniel. Much like Susanna, it will leave you spellbound—it was an important kind of God's power in the midst of a hostile environment. Idolatry was confronted and defeated in creative ways, exhibiting the hand of God—which is mighty against His enemies. The shrewd insight attributed to Daniel is indicative of his prophetic gift.

There you have a brief overview of these books commonly named the Deuterocanonical books. In the next few chapters, I will present a 28-day devotional that will direct you through various readings from both these books and the Old and New Testaments to show the common themes found throughout. Then my colleague, John, will return to help us further understand the historical context in which these books were written and read, and their impact on shaping the culture of first-century Palestine when Christ came on the scene proclaiming the kingdom of God.

Father Michael Pacella
Williamsburg, VA
February 2023

Chapter 1

The Sacred Books

Day 1

The Canon of Scripture

Today's Reading:
1 Timothy 3:15
2 Timothy 3:15-16
Sirach 38

The books that are included in the Bible are referred to as the Canon of Scripture, the books that were recognized by the Church as Spirit-inspired due to their authors and content. In selecting these books, Church Councils (both Universal and Ecumenical) established the doctrine of the divinity of Christ in 325 AD at Nicaea as well as the Councils of 431 AD at Ephesus and 451 AD at Chalcedon. The Councils also addressed the books to be recognized as worthy of inclusion in the Bible and they chose 72 or 73, a few more than the 66 that are commonly recognized today by evangelical and Protestant Christians.

Those seventy-plus books chosen were given fair consideration and were included based on their content as the Spirit directed. Paul wrote that the Church is the pillar of truth and the Word of God is its foundation for truth, and in these days the Church needs all the truth it can find to do its job of declaring truth and revealing Christ. It's important that you consider and even study not just the 66 books but the other so-called Apocryphal or Deuterocanonical books in their entirety.

1. Are you open to the fact that books in the Bible you have considered "extra" have worth for us today?

2. Have you read the Apocryphal books? Will you commit to do so in the coming days?

3. What can you do to become more knowledgeable where church history is concerned? Take a course? Do more reading?

Day 2

The Septuagint

Today's Bible reading:
Isaiah 7:14
Matthew 1:22-23

Most Christian people are unaware of the Bible translation Jesus, the apostles, and Paul would have used when they wrote and taught. It was called the Septuagint. Here is a little background. The world had been Hellenized, infiltrated by the Greek culture and customs, and many exiled Jews (for various reasons) were not in their homeland and thus could not read the Scriptures in their mother tongue, which was no longer Hebrew.

The library located in Alexandria, Egypt requested that the High Priest send scholars to translate the Jewish holy books into Greek. Of course, this then made the Septuagint the authorized version for Jews since Greek was the language of the world. It is referred to as the Septuagint because it is said that 70 scholars worked on the translation from Hebrew to Greek (*septa* is the Greek word for 70). This "miracle" translation was accomplished in record time and has been considered a monumental accomplishment for centuries.

1. Do more research on the history of the Septuagint.

2. Does it make sense that translating from one language to another is not always a word-for-word process, that sometimes concepts must be explained from one culture or language to another using more words than the original. Have you ever thought that this is the reason why Bible translations vary so widely? All the translators must make "judgment calls" when trying to convey certain topics or concepts.

3. Do you see how the early church would have drawn from a wide variety of early texts to teach the New Testament church since there was no one accepted list of holy books? Doesn't that then mean that some of those early texts could benefit modern believers as well?

Day 3

The Whole Counsel of God

Today's reading:
Hebrews 1:1-5
Isaiah 30:21
Wisdom 3

Is God confined to the Holy Scripture to speak to the world or can the Lord speak in other ways? No revelation should ever contradict sacred Scripture—however, God speaks to His people in various ways and in many places as Scripture reveals. The epitome of God's revelation is in the person of God's Son, Jesus Christ.

Circumstances are another way God uses to direct our steps—circumstances seem to be divinely arranged, so that we can walk in the path unobstructed. 'This is the way—walk ye in it'—a path has been unfolded for the obedient, and God is saying fear not! God knows all of His creatures and knows how to best communicate with each person. The conscience is another way of communicating love and guidance to each individual person.

God is a great communicator and is

sometimes subtle in the way He speaks, as stated above. One must be discerning before attributing to God a word from one's own heart. There are many warnings about this in holy Scripture. However, if God can speak through individuals and through history, why not through the Deuterocanonical books?

1. How has God communicated with you most effectively?

2. Does God communicate with His people through the various means mentioned above or is it solely through the sacraments and the Word?

3. Is there a situation now for which you are seeking God's wisdom? Are you expecting an answer?

Day 4

Meditating on the Scriptures

Today's Reading:
Matthew 21:29-42 (ESV)
John 10:35
Hebrews 11:35
Baruch 4

On many occasions, Jesus challenged His listeners to be committed to the word of God. One time, He asked learned Jews the question, "Have you never read?" and shocked the leaders when He told them they did not understand the Scriptures or the power of God. These were professional clerics who had devoted their lives to the study and application of Scripture. If Jesus had such a high view of Scripture, we should as well—and esteem *all* of it.

When Jesus spoke of the Scriptures which cannot be broken, to what was He referring? Did He know the parameters of the Scriptural corpus even though it not been established yet? When the Apostle Paul referred to "all Scripture," what did he have in mind? Did he use the Septuagint (LXX) as his source for citing Old Testament passages? If he did, then we know that it included more Old Testament books than our traditional Bibles have included.

1. What is your Bible reading plan?

2. Does it include the Deuterocanonical books?

3. How familiar are you with the Septuagint? Research its origins and usage.

Day 5

Biblical Sources

Today's Reading:
Jude in the New Testament
Baruch 1:14

Have you ever wondered the origin of some of the verses in the Bible that are in quotes but are not found in another book of your Bible? When I researched this, I found that some of the writers used historical books that had information about the times and customs of the day but were not included in the final canon of Scripture (notice especially Jude 9-11 and Jude 14-15).

> Yet the archangel Michael, when he argued with the devil in a dispute over the body of Moses, did not venture to pronounce a reviling judgment upon him but said, "May the Lord rebuke you!" But these people revile what they do not understand and are destroyed by what they know by nature like irrational animals. Woe to them! They followed the way of Cain, abandoned themselves to Balaam's error for the sake of gain, and perished in the rebellion of Korah (Jude 9-11).

Enoch, of the seventh generation from Adam, prophesied also about them when he said, "Behold, the Lord has come with his countless holy ones to execute judgment on all and to convict everyone for all the godless deeds that they committed and for all the harsh words godless sinners have uttered against him" (Jude 14-15).

If the authors of the Bible considered these sources valuable, then we should as well. They are worth reading, but they should never be mistaken as authoritative as regards to the formation of doctrine. They did, however, help contextualize the thoughts they were communicating when Jude, for example, told us about the battle for Moses' body, a story which the Old Testament did not reveal to us.

1. Are you open to learn new things about what you thought you knew that will expand your appreciation of God's word and Church history? Why or why not?

2. Do you have a reading program to gain more biblical knowledge? Are you open to asking someone for help in that area?

3. Do you have a reading program for your area of expertise and work (or ministry)? This may include returning to school or at least some kind of directed study program.

Day 6

Jesus and the Deuterocanonical Books

**Today's Reading:
See below**

In searching the Scriptures, I (Michael) detect approximately 400 Old Testament references in the book of Revelation. My point is that the New Testament is full of Old Testament references, including mention of images or concepts from the Deuterocanonical books. Consider these instances from the Gospels:

- slaying the holy innocents in Matthew 2:16; Herod's decree of slaying innocent children was prophesied in Wisdom 11:7.

- the role of spiritual fruit in identifying someone's spiritual condition in Matthew 7:16, 20; Jesus' statement "You will know them by their fruits" follows Sirach 27:6.

- sheep without a shepherd in Matthew

9:36; the people were "like sheep without a shepherd" as in Judith 11:19.

- The question concerning the seven brothers and the Resurrection in Matthew 22:25; Mark 12:20; and Luke 20:29; the gospel writers refer to the authenticity of Tobit 3:8 and 7:11.

- God the Father in John 5:18 where Jesus claimed that God is His Father; this corresponds with Wisdom 2:16.

- Falling on the edge of a sword in Luke 21:24; Jesus' usage of this phrase follows Sirach 28:18.

It would make sense that since these books were part of the Septuagint, Jesus would have been familiar with them and would naturally draw from them in His public ministry and teaching. If those books were part of our Lord's repertoire of resources, then they should be part of ours as well.

1. Take some time and do more research on all the other references to the Apocryphal books in the New Testament. Do you see the connections?

2. How much of your own culture do you find you have imposed on the Bible that was written centuries ago? Do you think this has affected your interpretation? What can you do to enter into the mindset of the writers themselves?

3. What can you do to better understand biblical history to help interpret the words of Jesus? Again, we would suggest reading and study.

Chapter 2

The Book of Tobit

Day 7

The Ways of God

Today's Reading:
Tobit 11
John 9:1-7

As we reflect on miracles in the Bible and the mystery of evil, the book of Tobit can help us understand the ways of God. The Lord Jesus brought about healing in "strange" ways, in one instance using mud made from His spit to heal a blind man's eyes. Therefore, there's no need to stumble over the unusual "miracles" in the book of Tobit.

As the people of God, we should expect "miracles" or the intervention of God in our everyday affairs and we should expect that some of them will defy natural description or comprehension. You are to live at all times in anticipation of the Holy Spirit's work as something on which you depend. You should live with reliance on the supernatural intervention of God as a Holy Spirit-led believer.

1. Do you have a story of a miraculous healing in your life or the life of someone close to you?

2. Do you believe God can and will heal you and others?

3. Have you ever stumbled over how God did something that was not according to how you thought He would do it? Describe the experience.

Day 8

Angels

Today's Reading:
Tobit 12:15-17
Hebrews 13:2

When I (Michael) was in Korea serving as an Army chaplain, two of my children told me they had separate angelic visitations while I was away. This may strike you as odd, but shouldn't it be the norm?

In the book of Tobit, the angel Raphael made a statement you saw in today's reading. The book of Hebrews reveals that some have entertained angels without being aware of it. Also, we saw that angels ministered to Jesus after His wilderness temptations, and He said He could summon angels to help Him just prior to His crucifixion. We are warned not to worship angels in Paul's letter to the Colossians and it is again reinforced in the book of Revelation, but we are told of their existence and their role as helpers of God's people.

It takes humility to admit that you need assistance from others, but it isn't weakness to ask assistance from God, your loving Father. In response to your cry, He may send angelic messengers as He did in the story in the book of Tobit.

1. Do you need help? Then call on Your heavenly Father!

2. Can you think of other instances in the Bible where God sent an angel when His people needed help? (The Christmas story is one such instance that comes to mind.)

3. Did you ever consider that God wants to use you as His messenger to assist others, just like He uses the angels? Are you open and available to that role?

Day 9

Your Children

Today's Reading:
Tobit 10
Luke 2:41-52

In both of today's readings, we read about anxious parents who thought they had lost a child. As a father who lost an adult child to a sudden death [Michael], I can relate to the anguish they must have felt. I certainly learned some important lessons through our loss. One of them was that the Lord gives and the Lord can take away, but blessed be the name of the Lord (see Job 1:21). Second, we discovered He is near the broken-hearted as He has promised (see Psalm 34:18). Finally, He will provide aid as you carry your cross of loss— mostly through friends and family, but sometimes through unexpected sources (see Matthew 27:32).

Parenthood is a close relationship whether the children are adopted (all our children [Michael] are adopted) or natural (our two are natural [John]). They go through stages in life and so do we as parents. We must be there the whole way through the journey with them, more as a source of counsel rather than as the voice of authority.

Tobit's parents were fretting over his delayed return but found that God had been protecting him through the presence of an angel. When my (Michael) son went off to war, I cried like a baby. However, I had no regrets because we had spent a lot of time with each other while he was growing up. He faced many dangerous situations and my wife and I prayed for him often. There comes a time when we need to trust the Lord and His holy angels for the safety of our children, especially if they're an only child.

1. If you have children, whose children are they? Do you rest in God's Fatherhood not only for you but also for your offspring?

2. Have you entrusted your children to the Lord to watch over and protect? Do you trust in His love for them?

3. Have you released your children to their divine destiny God has assigned for each one of them?

Chapter 3

The Book of Judith

Day 10

Women in Ministry

**Today's Reading:
Judith 8 and 13
Luke 1**

Judith is a wonderful example for women and men who are called to take great risks for God. She's part of a company of women God used throughout history to accomplish His will, women like Deborah in the book of Judges, Mary the mother of Jesus, Elizabeth the mother of John the Baptist, and the many women who assisted and led ministry outreaches during the time of the Apostle Paul. God did not call these women to be priests or prophets, but they wielded extraordinary power and influence before God and His people.

In Genesis 3:15, the Lord said, "I will put enmity between you and the woman, between your offspring and her offspring. She will crush your head, and you will lie in wait for her heel." This resembles a description of what Judith did when she cut off the head of Holofernes as found in Judith 13:8. The New Testament teaches that there is neither male nor female in Christ where purpose and service are concerned. God wants to use everyone in their sphere of competency and giftedness and that includes you—regardless of your gender.

1. How do you feel about women in ministry? Would you consider St. Joan of Arc and Mother Teresa as good examples of women who followed in the footsteps of Judith?

2. If God has given a woman a spiritual gift, shouldn't she be permitted to express it in the Church? Explain why or why not.

3. Do you know what your spiritual gifts are? How are you using them for the glory of God? Are you limiting yourself because of your age, gender, or level of education?

Day 11

Women of Honor

Today's Reading:
Esther 2
Psalm 139
Proverbs 31:10-31
Judith 10

God used the beauty of Esther and Judith to bring about His purposes at the time. He didn't exploit them, and they are good examples of how God prepares His chosen vessels to fulfill their purpose. In modern times when women are often objects of lust and exploited for evil means, we need examples of women who God used in a righteous manner.

These two women were spiritual women of great beauty *and* intelligence. Modern culture has at times downplayed the combination of those two characteristics but Esther and Judith embodied these excellent qualities. God knows we need these "models" of godliness to follow in these days of self-absorption and selfishness.

It's interesting that Esther's preparation in beauty school was for at least one year, for God wanted to make her even more of who He had already created her to be. All our beauty will fade away someday, but the inner beauty will endure forever. Let godly women follow these examples of courage, intelligence, and grace with the goal of allowing God to use every aspect of their being. And may we, like Esther, work diligently to be the best, fullest expression of who God created us to be.

1. Do you know your life purpose? Can you devote yourself to being the best you can be in the areas God has equipped you?

2. Psalm 139 says you are "fearfully and wonderfully made." Do you understand the implications that every aspect of your being emanated from the mind of God? What difference should this make in your work or ministry?

3. Esther was born for "such a time as this." What time were you born into? What's your unique contribution to the things of God in your generation?

Chapter 4

First and Second Maccabees

Day 12

Meet the Maccabees

Today's Reading:
Deuteronomy 31:1-32:47
1 Maccabees 1-3

Americans are not accustomed to hierarchy or the concept of royalty or nobility. However, in the Kingdom of God there are some who are considered champions or heroes because of their position and courage. Daniel and Joseph are good models of this reality because they remained godly in an ungodly environment, yet they had no clear successor so there was no one to whom they could hand off their leadership once it ended. And in the case of Moses, Joshua assumed leadership because he was God's choice. All of them, including the Maccabees, used their gifts and power for the common good.

Power is a force which only God can handle righteously. Humans tend to abuse power or often don't use it for the right reasons. Judas of the Maccabees, who was nicknamed the Hammer, was one who understood why God gives us power and how we should use it to the glory of God.

Judas assumed leadership after his father Mattathias' death and used his leadership power as he had seen his father deploy it, which was to benefit the nation and set God's people free from oppression. There we have a good example of leadership succession in a significant family in the Bible and it occurred not because they felt it was their right but because they served God and the people well—and they were prepared. God uses those who are prepared to be used!

1. What you doing with any leadership power you have? Are you growing in your ability to handle power?

2. Have you seen leadership succession plans go awry in your life and work? Why did they fail?

3. If you are a leader, what are you doing about leadership succession? If not a leader, can you think of a good example of someone who is addressing the succession issue (or not)?

Day 13

His-Story

Today's Reading:
2 Maccabees 2
Acts 7

Stephen, the first martyr of the New Testament Church, recounted the history of Israel precisely and with finesse when he faced his enemies before they put him to death. We also must know our story—which is His-story or history. We should be able to recount it with accuracy, whether it's the story of the parting of the Red Sea or other great miracles God has done on behalf of His covenant people as recorded in both the Old and New Testaments.

The beautiful thing about the Bible is that it doesn't gloss over the imperfections or failures in the lives of its "saints." There's no superficial veneer applied to make them look like they received well-deserved halos. We get the whole picture of who they were and what they did, wrinkles and all. Yet, God in His infinite mercy used them all in powerful and effective ways.

It's important that we be connected to our spiritual heritage and know it thoroughly and by heart. That's the reason the story of the Maccabees isn't just part of Jewish heritage but also part of the Church's as well. You need to know your God and His works in the earth and draw encouragement from their testimony of His great faithfulness. Declare them from the housetops, so others can learn about His mighty deeds, and then do some mighty deeds yourself.

1. Who are your favorite heroes in the Bible? What lessons are you learning from them that you can apply to your own life?

2. Who are your favorite heroes in Church history outside the Bible? What lessons are you learning from them that you can apply to your own life?

3. Are you allowing your imperfections and failures to hinder how God can and wants to use you? How can you be freed from unrealistic expectations of yourself to serve Him more effectively as you are and not as you think you should be or others want you to be?

Day 14

Conform or Transform?

Today's reading:
Romans 12:1-2
Daniel 1
2 Maccabees 6

The Maccabees faced what the Church is facing today, which is how much we have come to resemble the surrounding culture as modern values influence believers to conform to their standards. The Maccabees refused to eat the king's meat and it cost some of them their lives. Daniel and his friends did the same but God spared and promoted them. The point is that all had reached a point where they said "enough is enough" and they took a stand for righteousness' sake.

Paul addressed this dilemma with the simple admonition that we are not to be conformed to culture's standards but to be transformed by the renewing of our minds. We need to draw from the examples of both Daniel and the Maccabees (specifically Eleazar) and refuse to partake of anything that may prevent us from "digesting" God's words or following His ways as we were warned about doing in Proverbs 23:1-3: "When you sit to dine with a ruler, note well what is before you, and put a knife to your throat if you are given to gluttony. Do not crave his delicacies, for that food is deceptive."

The Church should have a distinctive culture when others observe it. Its language and conduct should be somewhat peculiar to the outsider but perfectly normal to people of faith. This distinction has always been a mark of God's people, who are a holy people and a royal priesthood.

1. Why do you think believers are at times afraid to be different? How do we balance being different without being weird? How can we be unique but still accessible or relevant to those who are outside the church?

2. Are there any areas which you have compromised that have impacted your witness?

3. Where are you being pressured to eat the "king's meat"? What can you learn from Daniel or the Maccabees about taking a stand for God?

Day 15

God's Heroes

Today's Reading:
2 Maccabees 7
Hebrews 11:32-40

The people of God should acknowledge and learn from the moving historical accounts found in 1 and 2 Maccabees. We should admire and seek to emulate their heroic examples of commitment and dedication as people who faced death but still stood strong for God. Hanukkah commemorates the rededication of the Temple in 165 BC by the Maccabees after its desecration by the Syrians, and is celebrated by Jews to this day. This miraculous intervention refutes the concept that God was not speaking or acting in the four centuries between Malachi of the Old Testament and the Gospel of Matthew in the New Testament.

The sacrifice and torture that our forebearers endured should encourage us to be bold in our generation regarding our witness and testimony. I refer especially to 2 Maccabees 7 where it states in verse 41, "Then, last of all, after the sons, the mother also was consumed." The whole family gave their lives in the hope of a future resurrection, spurred on by their noble mother, who also sacrificed her life for the truth of God's word. These heroes (and God knows we need heroes in today's world) are the best examples we have in Hebrew history of true death-defying courage, along with many outstanding stories in the book of Daniel (along with its Greek extensions—to be explained in a future entry).

1. Do you know the full story behind what Jews celebrate during Hanukkah? Perhaps you should find out.

2. Who are your heroes of the faith, either in the Bible or from historical accounts? What impresses you most about their lives or example?

3. Do you have what it takes to be a faith hero?

Chapter 5

Esther with the Greek Extension

Day 16

The God of (and in) Esther

Today's Reading:
The Book of Esther with the Greek extension
Hebrews 11:31-34

Esther is an important book in the corpus of Holy Writ, yet many maintain that the book should not be included in the canon of Scripture because the name of God is not used or mentioned in it. However, the version with the Greek extension mentions God fifty times, making this so-called "secular" or non-God book a God-centered one.

Mordecai and Esther were God-fearing people who obeyed God's law and engaged in godly practices like fasting and prayer. Therefore, it would not be logical to think they did not have or did not operate from a Hebrew or God-honoring perspective. Esther's book can't be properly understood without the godly worldview the extended Greek version provides.

1. Do you have a worldview that includes God, the condition of the world, and the remedy for it through Christ? Do you live this worldview? Can you explain and defend it?

2. Like Esther, you were born for such a time as this. Do you know your purpose?

3. Are you facing a dilemma in your life or work? If so, perhaps it's time to pray and fast like Esther, Mordecai, and other Jews did, realizing that God chose you to serve Him in such a time as this.

Day 17

Crying Out To God

Today's Reading:
Esther 12:14-16, 23-25
Exodus 2:1-10

This prayer in the Greek extension reveals a more comprehensive understanding of the spiritual life of Esther. I (Michael) was watching a movie titled *Soul Surfer* which was the story of a young girl who was a surfing champion but who lost most of her left arm during a shark attack. However, she was still able to compete at a high level after her recovery. It's reported that those writing the script wanted to take out all references to God and faith but the parents of the champion refused to consent. They knew faith in God was part-and-parcel with the story and could not be eliminated.

The story of Esther is similar in that we can't read or understand it without the spiritual component being revealed and included. We can't secularize this important biblical story that tells us of the intervention of God and a woman's intercession in God's plan. What's more, Esther's success should not be separated from what had to be a vibrant faith and prayer life that led her to turn to God in a time of trouble.

1. Do you involve God in every aspect of your life, not just church but also work, family, studies, and social life?

2. Are other people being impacted by your prayers and fasting? In other words, are your spiritual disciplines finding an expression in your life and work?

3. Are you part of a team with whom you regularly pray and who will pray for you as you do for them, even when you're not physically together?

Chapter 6

Daniel with the Greek Extension

Day 18

Young Daniel

Today's Reading:
Daniel 1 with the Greek Extension
1 Samuel 10:21-22
1 Samuel 17

The first chapter of the book of Daniel in the Greek extension relates the story of Susannah who was accused by two elders of being unfaithful to her husband through an adulterous affair in her garden— supposedly observed by the accusing elders. She was speedily convicted because of the position and status of her accusers and was condemned to death.

Daniel appeared on the scene and astutely questioned the elders separately as to what tree the affair took place under. They both gave different versions and were found to be lying because of their own lust and desire for Susannah. (They even insisted that during the trial her face remain uncovered so they could behold her beauty.) It was then that the people realized Daniel had the gift of prophecy and discernment and was invited to sit among the elders of God's people. I recommend that you read this inspiring story and see God's justice firsthand being demonstrated by a young man with a prophetic gift.

1. Do you know your spiritual gifts like Daniel knew his? Do you use them for the benefit of others? Do others recognize them as well?

2. Do you recognize those around you who have the ability to hear from God and communicate what they hear? Who are they? Do you have such a gift?

3. Are you quick to jump to conclusions before hearing all sides of a story? Can you think of a time when you did not? What were the circumstances and results of this rush to judgment?

Day 19

Bel and the Dragon

Today's Reading:
Daniel 13:1-14:42
Hebrews 11:33-34

The stories of Susanna and of Bel and the Dragon were collected by the Greek translators from a body of Daniel traditions and incorporated into the book of Daniel as an appendix. The Catholic Church has defined them to be a part of the canonical Scriptures. Bel was one of the names of Marduk, the patron divinity of Babylon. There's ample evidence of serpent-worship in Babylon, but no evidence that living serpents were worshiped as gods.

Bel and the Dragon is an intriguing and interesting account of the wisdom of God working through the prophet Daniel. It's an important account of the power of God working in a hostile spiritual environment. Idolatry was confronted and defeated in creative ways, demonstrating the hand of God—which has always been mighty for His people against their enemies. The shrewd insight attributed to Daniel is indicative of his prophetic gift.

1. Daniel received practical wisdom to address a spiritual problem in his day. Are you available to the Lord to serve the same role in your current life and work?

2. What feedback do you receive from people that can help you understand your role and gifts God has assigned you? Be specific.

3. Are you hiding in the church or are you available for Him to use you in and outside the church to confront serious spiritual problems?

Day 20

Praying in the Furnace of Affliction

Today's Reading:
Daniel 3 in the Greek Extension
Daniel 3 in the Protestant Bible

There is no more gripping story in the Bible than of the three young men who refused to bow down and worship the image Nebuchadnezzar had created after Daniel interpreted the king's dreams. In the Greek extension, we find a prayer that one of the men prayed that isn't in the Bible you use. We urge you to read this portion of Daniel 3 to be inspired by such words from a man in a time of great affliction and danger.

1. If you want to pray inspired prayers, then model your prayers after those found in God's word. What part of Azariah's prayer can you use in your own prayer life?

2. What other prayers found in the Bible can you begin to use in your devotions? Keep in mind that the psalms are to a great extent a collection of prayers.

3. Do you ever write out your prayers? Consider doing this as part of your journaling or social media presence to share with others so they can pray along with you.

Chapter 7

The Letter of Baruch

Day 21

Context

Today's Reading:
Baruch 1-5
Jeremiah 51:31-35

Baruch, the scribe for the prophet Jeremiah, is said to have left behind a letter clarifying the works of God as he observed them during the days of the prophet. This makes Baruch's letter especially important, for it provides more background to help us better understand the ministry challenges and context of Jeremiah's ministry. Another example of a ministry relationship like this is Luke and his relationship to Paul, which enabled Luke to provide valuable context and insight into the work of Paul at the time he was in ministry.

History tells us that the Apostle Peter was the source of information for John Mark when he wrote the Gospel of Mark. St. Prochorus is said to have been the scribe for the Apostle John the Theologian, as he is referred to in church history. All these relationships are important and revealing, which is the reason Baruch's letter is so significant for us today.

1. What can you do to increase your awareness of church history?

2. Are you in a position to assist a leader in their role? How can you do so?

3. If you are a leader, do you have trusted associates who can assist you?

Day 22

Worthy Successors

Today's reading:
Baruch (all)
2 Timothy 2:2

I [Michael] am enamored with the writings of the Apostolic fathers who sat at the feet of the original Apostles and were their appointed successors as bishops. From what better sources could we draw wisdom and insight than these key figures in the early church? The New Testament teaches that God has placed first the apostles (think of them as army generals) than prophets and then teachers in the body of Christ for building up and equipping the saints as described in 1 Corinthians 12:28. This list isn't meant to minimize the other important gifts of the Spirit to the Church. However, this continuity of leadership roles is important so we can understand the centuries-old culture in which the books of the Bible were written.

St. John the Apostle, according to church history, used St. Prochorus as his scribe. St. Peter used St. Mark who wrote the Gospel of Mark.

They chose assistants who would not take liberties with their work, but instead looked for those who would revere it as the word of God and not the word of humans. Someone with this sensitivity would not write something on their own without first receiving revelation and inspiration from God—they would fear God and honor their mentors too deeply to act recklessly.

This leads to my conclusion about the importance we should attach to the book of Baruch. He was there—a firsthand witness of the times and trials of the prophet Jeremiah. He knew Jeremiah and was chosen to record important historical events which would indicate he was considered trustworthy by the Lord and Jeremiah. We should want to know all we can of the background for any of God's leaders so we can understand and apply their teaching from Him more accurately and effectively.

1. Are you a faithful messenger? By that, we mean are you faithful to pass on what you have learned exactly as you have learned it to others?

2. Are you imparting what you know and do to others who can transmit it to others once you have gone on to your heavenly reward?

3. Do you look for natural human elements that make the Bible come alive and relevant or are you tied to a narrow view of Scripture and its creation?

Chapter
8

Wisdom
of
Solomon

Day 23

Being Wise

Today's reading:
Wisdom of Solomon 9
Proverbs 8
1 Corinthians 1:30

The Wisdom of Solomon complements the Wisdom Literature of the Old Testament (or as some prefer to call it, the First Testament). The current moral state of the world and the Church indicates that we can't afford to ignore any of God's wisdom wherever it's found, which makes all the Wisdom books important. All truth is God's truth.

We need wisdom not only in the form of rules, but also in how and where to apply true knowledge as we learn and digest it. The sages of Jewish history have left us nuggets of wisdom in a practical framework, including books like the Wisdom of Solomon. We would be wise to heed its content. There are no shortcuts to wisdom and knowledge. The Holy Spirit can't do the work that only you can do and that includes study, application, reflection, feedback, and correction.

Scripture teaches that we should not move the ancient boundaries (see Proverbs 22:28), but instead should adhere to the parameters established by God in all His word and the historical documents and precedents of the Church.

1. What are you doing to grow in wisdom and knowledge? Do you have a plan?

2. What are you doing to grow in an understanding of biblical and Church history?

3. If you are wise, what do you do to make that wisdom available for the good of others? Consider writing and teaching as possible outlets to accomplish this.

Day 24

Wisdom's Fruit

Today's reading:
Wisdom of Solomon 10
1 Kings 4
1 Kings 10

It's moving to read Solomon's prayer as a young man asking to receive wisdom instead of power, riches, or victory over his enemies. God honored his prayer and gave him great wisdom— along with all the other things he could have asked for but did not. This wisdom had practical expressions as found in 1 Kings 4 and 10. People from all over the world came to hear him lecture on nature, relationships, and righteousness. What's more, Solomon composed more than 1,000 songs and wrote in excess of 3,000 proverbial sayings.

Don't you think that Solomon produced so much and touched so many lives that it would be difficult to contain it all in one book of the Bible named Proverbs? That's why it makes perfect sense that there are other books, one of which is named after him. We would do well to study anything that was remotely connected to the wisest man who ever walked the face of the earth—next to Jesus—even if that wisdom was delivered by those who sat at his feet and gave him credit for what they wrote.

As we seek wisdom, however, we should be humbled to see the result in Solomon's life, which wasn't a model for righteous behavior. Wisdom can't be an end unto itself but must always be connected to the practical expression of ethics and moral living as God would desire and the Scriptures clearly teach.

1. What is wisdom in its essence and how is it best expressed? Name some good models for wisdom in the Bible or from history.

2. How can you walk with these models so you can learn and grow in wisdom?

3. What practical creative expressions do you have that God has given you to help you express your wisdom? Writing? Arts and crafts? Painting? Science? Medicine?

Chapter 9

The Book
of Sirach or
Ecclesiasticus

Day 25

Age-Old Wisdom

Today's reading:
Sirach 13
Proverbs 5

American culture often cherishes and values knowledge more than it does wisdom. Sages are not esteemed because Western cultures are sometimes enamored with youth and therefore the elderly are regarded as outdated and useless. I [Michael] never met any of my grandparents who all died before I was born except one (who was looked upon as not being a good example for children). I felt like I missed out on the wisdom they should have acquired over the years and imparted to me. I also drew little wisdom from my parents' lives other than realizing that I should not do some of the things they did. So where does one go for wisdom? Where was I to go? I went to the Bible.

There is a corpus of writing in the Bible that is categorized as Wisdom Literature. It's made up of various collections of wise sayings which can help a young or old person navigate the challenging times in their lives. Anyone who wants to live a successful life and leave a noble legacy must work to do so. It doesn't just happen because they are nice people. We all must have the right tools if we are to live a successful and abundant life in the Aristotelian sense, which is defined as flourishing or reaching one's potential. Those tools are available to us all in the Wisdom Literature which is plentiful in the Deuterocanonical books of Ecclesiasticus or Sirach and Wisdom of Solomon.

1. What are your sources of wisdom for living? Who or what gives you the insight you need to thrive at what you do and who you are?

2. Are you flourishing or just existing? Explain your answer.

3. Do you desire to grow your wisdom, apply it, and then share it? Describe your strategy where wisdom is concerned. (For example, I [John] have studied the book of Proverbs my entire adult life and have written two daily devotionals from what I learned.)

Day 26

Wisdom for Every Age

Today's Reading:
Sirach Prologue and Chapter 1
Proverbs 1

The ethics adopted by Western civilization has its roots in the Decalogue (The Ten Commandments) of the Hebrew Scriptures. Tradition tells us that the sages didn't recommend that anyone under the age of fifty read the book of Ezekiel. On the other hand, Sirach contains wisdom for young and old alike because it is a handbook that covers a broad scope of practical life issues. Sirach elaborates on these important values and virtues. Sirach is a long book but is a useful tool for the young and old alike. Philosophers and theologians through the ages have posed the question, "How shall we live?" Sirach's manual answers that question and goes on to provide concrete instruction and virtuous guidance.

1. Do you journal your thoughts and insights? This is an important practice if you are going to learn and grow in wisdom.

2. What specific wisdom do you need? For family? Ministry? Work? Finances? What's your plan to get the wisdom you need?

3. How are you sharing the wisdom you gain? Writing? Teaching? Social media? Family devotions?

Day 27

Wisdom for Life

Today's reading:
Proverbs 31:1-6
Ecclesiasticus 38

I [Michael] remember reading about hydro-planing in my driver's manual. I passed my driver's test, but I didn't learn wisdom where hydroplaning was concerned until I was able to handle that dangerous situation in real life. How about another illustration? A man was given a line in a play which read—"Hark the cannon roars"—it was his only line so he expressed it in many ways before the dress rehearsal. When the cannon went off in dress rehearsal, however, instead of saying his line, "Hark the cannon roars," he said, "What the heck was that?" Knowledge is one thing—wisdom is quite another.

In Ecclesiasticus, we have an unusual passage that addresses the God-given role of doctors and how He uses them to do His healing work. The writer directed us that if we are sick, we are to pray and repent, but also to consult with our physician. He goes to give other practical advice about life's challenges. I would not have expected that advice from a spiritual writer, but it shows how God wants to be involved in every aspect of our lives—and that prayer and faith are not the answer to everything. We need to make use of all God's means for life and health.

I love all the Wisdom Literature and find it helpful in my everyday journey with the Lord. The practical advice given in these documents will prove to be a special blessing for those who did not have a godly father or a mother like King Lemuel as recorded in Proverbs 31. Even those who have had this advantage will be able to re-inforce the many lessons they learned at the feet of godly parents. However, for the rest of us—we need all the help we can get!

1. Is there a contradiction in going to the doctor and still having faith in God for your healing? If not, why not? If you are healed by medical means, did the Lord still heal you?

2. Do you see the hand of God healing others through nature and natural means as well as chemical and medical means?

3. What are you doing to grow your wisdom? Is it only spiritual or is your wisdom useful for practical issues of life as well?

Day 28

The Mystery of Death

Today's reading:
Wisdom 3
2 Maccabees 7
Matthew 6:19-24

At a recent funeral where I [Michael] offici-
ated, the deacon chose the reading from Wisdom
3 while I chose and read a gospels' text. Look
again at part of what you read for today's assigned
reading:

> The souls of the righteous are in the hand
> of God, and no torment shall touch them.
> They seemed, in the view of the foolish,
> to be dead; and their passing away was
> thought an affliction and their going
> forth from us, utter destruction. But they
> are in peace. For if to others, indeed, they
> seem punished, yet is their hope full of
> immortality; chastised a little, they shall
> be greatly blessed, because God tried
> them and found them worthy of himself.
> As gold in the furnace, he proved them,

and as sacrificial offerings he took them to himself. In the time of their judgment they shall shine and dart about as sparks through stubble; they shall judge nations and rule over peoples, and the Lord shall be their King forever. Those who trust in him shall understand truth, and the faithful shall abide with him in love: because grace and mercy are with his holy ones, and his care is with the elect (Wisdom 3:1-9).

I don't know of a more compelling and courageous story of a godly family in Holy Writ than the story found in 2 Maccabees 7. They embraced death, not as the end, but as a path to another life and invested their life in this world trusting that it was not the end, but only the gateway to a new beginning. Take some time to review its contents in an attempt to understand the mystery of death.

1. Are you aware that you are a pilgrim, just passing through this life to the next? What implications should that have for how you live now?

2. Death is the gateway to that next life. How can you prepare for it now? (Hint: Read Matthew 6:19-24 for some direction.)

3. First Corinthians 15:55 asks where are death's sting and victory. What did Paul mean? How should a Christian approach death as opposed to someone who does not know the Lord?

Chapter 10

The Inter-Testament Period Between Malachi and Matthew

John Stanko

My thanks to Father Michael for this wonderful overview involving devotionals that drew from all the books of the Bible including the Apocryphal entries. In this chapter, let's revisit some of the historical concepts Father Michael and I mentioned earlier in this book. This is important for it gives the modern reader a much fuller context to understand the dynamics of Jesus as He preached and taught Jews who had been shaped by historical, political, and cultural influences—many of which are alluded to and described in the Apocrypha.

The Sadducees

Let's start out by looking at the religious leaders who existed at the time of Jesus and were named the Sadducees. Here's what author Charles Pfeiffer (1959) had to say about this group:

> Although the Pharisees and Sadducees are frequently denounced together in the New Testament, they had little in common save their antagonism to Jesus.
>
> The Sadducees were the party of the Jerusalem aristocracy and the high priesthood. They had made their peace with the political rulers and had attained positions of wealth and influence. Temple administration and ritual was their specific responsibility. In the later Hasmonean period and the Roman period which followed it, the high priesthood had become a political football so that the religious interests of the office tended to be pushed into the background. The Sadducees themselves remained aloof from the masses and were unpopular with them.
>
> Theologically the Sadducees must be

described with a series of negatives. They did not accept the oral law which developed under the Pharisees, and seem to have limited their canon to the Torah, or Pentateuch. They did not believe in the resurrection, spirits, or angels (cf. Mark 12:18; Luke 20:27; Acts 23:8). They left no positive religious or theological system.

The Pharisees welcomed and made proselytes (cf. Matthew 23:15), but the Saducean party was closed. None but the members of the High Priestly and aristocratic families of Jerusalem could be Sadducees. With the destruction of the Jerusalem temple in AD 70, the Sadducees came to an end. Modern Judaism traces its roots to the party of the Pharisees (p. 115).

One of the most telling and breathtaking encounters Jesus had with the Sadducees is described in Matthew's gospel. Father Michael has already shared that the influence on Jesus lesson in this encounter probably came from the Apocryphal book of Tobit:

That same day the Sadducees, who say there is no resurrection, came to him with a question. "Teacher," they said, "Moses told us that if a man dies without having children, his brother must marry the widow and raise up offspring for him. Now there were seven brothers among us. The first one married and died, and since he had no children, he left his wife to his brother. The same thing happened to the second and third brother, right on down to the seventh. Finally, the woman died. Now then, at the resurrection, whose wife will she be of the seven, since all of them were married to her?"

Jesus replied, "You are in error because you do not know the Scriptures or the power of God. At the resurrection people will neither marry nor be given in marriage; they will be like the angels in heaven. But about the resurrection of the dead—have you not read what God said to you, 'I am the God of Abraham, the God of Isaac, and the God of Jacob'? He is not the God of the dead but of the living."

When the crowds heard this, they were astonished at his teaching (Matthew 22:23-33, NIV).

Jesus told these men who were the high priestly family that they did not know the Scriptures or the power of God. They had become so political that they had restricted their biblical interests to such a limited extent that they didn't believe in much of anything, except their ability to maintain power through their tenuous alliance with Rome.

Why is this important for our study of the Apocrypha? It indicates the spiritual condition of Jesus' contemporaries, which was a far cry from their condition described in the Apocryphal books we have examined. Those centuries prior to Jesus' coming were not silent years; they were years of vibrant faith when God walked closely with His people. When Jesus came, He announced the coming of the Kingdom the people had been longing for, but not according to the expectations they had of a political, powerful monarch who would establish the Jews' supremacy over all other people groups.

The Pharisees

Now let's consider the other religious group

in Jesus' day known as the Pharisees. The very mention of that name causes the hair on our theological and biblical necks to stand up. These were the men who on many occasions opposed Jesus and who eventually conspired with the Sadducees to put Him to death. They were a sect or movement of Puritans who wanted to preserve the traditions of their fathers and maintain a strict moral code based on the Torah or Law of God.

Who were these men? How did they get to be who and what they were? What exactly did they stand for and why? The reason I raise this is because the Apocrypha and the history it represents shed much light and help us to answer the questions I just raised.

Today, we read the heated encounter that Jesus had with the Pharisees in Matthew 23 and wonder how they got to this point in their history where they incurred God's anger. To answer that, let's start by reading Matthew 23 in its entirety:

> Then Jesus said to the crowds and to his disciples: "The teachers of the law and the Pharisees sit in Moses' seat. So you must be careful to do everything they tell you. But do not do what they do, for they do not practice what they preach. They tie up heavy, cumbersome loads and put them on other people's shoulders, but they themselves are not willing to lift a finger to move them.

> "Everything they do is done for people to see: They make their phylacteries[a] wide and the tassels on their garments long; they love the place of honor at banquets and the most important seats in the synagogues; they love to be greeted with respect in the marketplaces and to be called 'Rabbi' by others.

"But you are not to be called 'Rabbi,' for you have one Teacher, and you are all brothers. And do not call anyone on earth 'father,' for you have one Father, and he is in heaven. Nor are you to be called instructors, for you have one Instructor, the Messiah. The greatest among you will be your servant. For those who exalt themselves will be humbled, and those who humble themselves will be exalted.

"Woe to you, teachers of the law and Pharisees, you hypocrites! You shut the door of the kingdom of heaven in people's faces. You yourselves do not enter, nor will you let those enter who are trying to.

"Woe to you, teachers of the law and Pharisees, you hypocrites! You travel over land and sea to win a single convert, and when you have succeeded, you make them twice as much a child of hell as you are.

"Woe to you, blind guides! You say, 'If anyone swears by the temple, it means nothing; but anyone who swears by the gold of the temple is bound by that oath.' You blind fools! Which is greater: the gold, or the temple that makes the gold sacred? You also say, 'If anyone swears by the altar, it means nothing; but anyone who swears by the gift on the altar is bound by that oath.' You blind men! Which is greater: the gift, or the altar that makes the gift sacred? Therefore, anyone who swears by the altar swears by it and by everything on it. And anyone who swears by the temple swears by it and by the one who dwells in it. And anyone who swears by heaven swears by God's throne and by the one who sits on it.

"Woe to you, teachers of the law and Pharisees, you hypocrites! You give a tenth of your spices—mint, dill and cumin. But you have neglected the more important matters of the law—justice, mercy and faithfulness. You should have practiced the latter, without neglecting the former. You blind guides! You strain out a gnat but swallow a camel.

"Woe to you, teachers of the law and Pharisees, you hypocrites! You clean the outside of the cup and dish, but inside they are full of greed and self-indulgence. [26] Blind Pharisee! First clean the inside of the cup and dish, and then the outside also will be clean.

"Woe to you, teachers of the law and Pharisees, you hypocrites! You are like whitewashed tombs, which look beautiful on the outside but on the inside are full of the bones of the dead and everything unclean. In the same way, on the outside you appear to people as righteous but on the inside you are full of hypocrisy and wickedness.

"Woe to you, teachers of the law and Pharisees, you hypocrites! You build tombs for the prophets and decorate the graves of the righteous. And you say, 'If we had lived in the days of our ancestors, we would not have taken part with them in shedding the blood of the prophets.' So you testify against yourselves that you are the descendants of those who murdered the prophets. Go ahead, then, and complete what your ancestors started!

"You snakes! You brood of vipers! How will you escape being condemned to hell? Therefore I am sending you prophets and sages and teachers. Some of them you will kill and crucify; others you will flog in your synagogues and pursue from town to town. And so upon you will come all the righteous blood that has been shed on earth, from the blood of righteous Abel to the blood of Zechariah son of Berekiah, whom you murdered between the temple and the altar. Truly I tell you, all this will come on this generation.

"Jerusalem, Jerusalem, you who kill the prophets and stone those sent to you, how often I have longed to gather your children together, as a hen gathers her chicks under her wings, and you were not willing. Look, your house is left to you desolate. For I tell you, you will not see me again until you say, 'Blessed is he who comes in the name of the Lord'" (NIV).

How could God have moved so mightily on behalf of the people in the period of the Maccabees, only 150 years later to pronounce judgment on them and their religious values and house of worship? Rather than try to answer that on my own, I would like to quote a passage from a series of sermons by the British "prince of expositors," G. Campbell Morgan, who addressed the issue of the Pharisees in one of his published sermons. Then I will make some additional comments.

I think we shall be very unfair to the meaning of our Master if we begin in the 23rd chapter of Matthew, that chapter from which I read one extract in connection with our lesson, that chapter vibrant with the thunder of His [Jesus] awful woes against these very men. I think we must not begin there. I think we very often miss the keen edge of what Jesus said by beginning at the wrong place.

Where, then, shall we begin? Let us ask who these Pharisees were. The answer to the inquiry may be thus stated: The Pharisees were the Puritans of the Maccabean period in Jewish history. Their very name means *separated ones*, and I do no violence to the name "Pharisee" when I say it means Separatist. That is precisely what they were. We have no history of the actual period in our Bible, but we have the history of its beginning in the books of Ezra and Nehemiah, and we have revelations of the conditions in the books of Haggai, Zachariah, and Malachi. God's ancient people, or a remnant of them, were established in Jerusalem, without any king or prophet. There originated the order of the Scribes of which Ezra was the first.

As time proceeded these people were threatened with complete absorption by the Greek power that swept over that whole region, and in that period, of which we have no biblical history, but of which we have a good deal of authentic history, Judas Maccabeus became the deliverer of the people. There was a period of victories, and these Hebrew people suffered as a result, for they were in danger of forming alliances with the surrounding peoples and of being corrupted by the Greek influence which stood in direct opposition to their own conception of God and religion.

It was then, when, humanly speaking, the Hebrew people were threatened with that most terrible form of extinction—absorption—that the Pharisees arose. The passion which actuated those who found the order was one of loyalty to Jehovah. They constituted themselves into a definite order. I think when we read the New Testament we sometimes forget that the Pharisees were members of a very definite order. There were not more than six- or seven-thousand of them. The order was a closed religious corporation. They banded themselves together as men who would be entirely separated from the Gentiles, from those whom they described as the common people, that is, those who did not take those special religious vows, and especially from the Sadducees, who were the rationalists in religion.

The movement was born of the highest, holiest passion. The order of the Pharisees was an order of men who stood for purity in religion in an hour when Hebraism was threatened by contamination by Greek influence, which would have cut the nerve of the religion of Jehovah. There can be no question, and those who are most familiar with the history of those times will agree with me, that they were the saviors of the nation, the men who enabled that remnant to stand against the encroachment of the forces of worldliness that were sweeping

down on the people. These were the
Pharisees, and these were the men with
whom Jesus Christ was brought into im-
mediate contact, when he began his public teaching .

From the commencement of His public
ministry to the close we see him flinging
Himself with all the force of His per-
sonality against them and against their
teaching. How are we to account for this?
Let us look at them again. Let us see what
had happened to them in the course of
the years, not tracing the movement but
seeing the result as it is revealed to us in
the New Testament. What had their righteousness become? Let us inquire what
was the base of it and examine the structure of it in order that we may understand the failure and insufficiency of it.

What was the base of the righteousness
which the Pharisees taught? Conformity
to the will of God. When you speak of
the Pharisees, remember that they were
the most religious people of that period.
They were the most orthodox, the men
who stood by the old theology. No one
will imagine I am condemning ortho-
doxy, or sneering at old theology.

When we come into the Acts of the
Apostles, we find that the opposition
was not Pharisaic, but Sadducean. So
long as Jesus was teaching morality, the
Sadducees had no quarrel with him; they
were indifferent; it was the resurrection
doctrine they put the Sadducees into opposition with Christ. The Pharisees were
religious, orthodox, and the base of their
morality was their belief that man must

conform to the will of God. Wherein, then, lay there failure? In order to answer that question, let us observe the structure which they had built on that base. Three things characterize their righteousness: it was, first, external; second, it was exclusive; finally, therefore, it was evasive of essential righteousness.

It was, first, external. It consisted in a most complex and elaborate system of regulations of life by habits. As every man entered the order he took two vows of initiation. The first was the tithe everything eaten, bought, or sold. The second was not to be the guest of the Gentiles, and to observe all ceremonial purifications. These were the fundamental vows of initiation to the order of the Pharisees. Now observe what had happened in the process of the years. In their desire to interpret the law of God and to make it binding, they had added tradition to tradition. A little careful study of the Pharisees reveals things that are almost too absurd to be mentioned.

Here is one simple illustration of their traditions. If a man should walk through the cornfields on the Sabbath day, he must wear the lightest sandals, as if he were heavy ones and trod on the corn and thus forced it from its husk, he was threshing on the Sabbath! You smile at that, but I know puritanism today which is quite as foolish! They attempted to explain the meaning of the thought of God by their own foolish tradition until they had heaped tradition upon tradition, and the Lord said to them, "They bind heavy burdens and grievous to be borne, and lay them on men's shoulders; but they themselves will not move them with their fingers."

Moreover, their righteousness was exclusive. They held in supreme contempt all who were outside their own order. In the New Testament we become quite familiar with their attitude toward the publican. That phrase, the "common people," in itself full of beauty because it describes, not the people of one class or caste, but all sorts of people, when used by the Pharisees included all those who were not Pharisees, learned and illiterate, rich and poor, bond and free, the common herd outside the Pharisaic order, on all of whom the Pharisees looked with profound contempt.

Notice another revelation of the exclusiveness of the Pharisee, and I shall reveal what is in my mind by again quoting from the words of Jesus, "Ye compass sea and land to make one proselyte: and when he is become so, you make him two fold more a son of hell than yourselves." There is no stronger proof of exclusivism than the passion and desire to proselytize someone else and bring that other person to your view. You reveal your exclusivism in no surer away than when you attempt to take hold of the man you hold in contempt because he is not with you, and compel him to your way of thinking.

Finally, their righteousness was evasive. Accentuation of the letter had destroyed the spirit. The Sabbath was held so sacred that if the observance of its hallowed sanctions were denied, so that when His disciples passed through the cornfields and plucked the ears of corn the Pharisees complained that they were breaking the Sabbath, and Jesus said, "If ye had known what this means, I desire mercy, and not sacrifice, he would not have condemned the guiltless." Have you ever really examined that answer of Jesus? These men were insisting on the sanctity of the Sabbath in such a way as to harm humanity, and Christ swept their traditions away, declaring that even the sanctity of the sun above must give way to the sanction of caring for humanity. They would not work on the Sabbath, but they would hold their feasts on the Sabbath, provided Gentiles prepared them. Consequently, I repeat, the very accentuation of the value of the letter had destroyed the spirit.

Wherein, then, lay the failure of these men? What was wrong? If the base of their righteousness was the conviction that righteousness is conformity to the will of God, wherein were they wrong? In that they did not know God. Consequently, they were unequal to the interpretation of the will of God. They did not understand the nature of His holiness. They did not understand the nature of His love. Out of that ignorance of God they proceeded to attempt to bring men into conformity to the will of the God whom they did not know, and whose will therefore they did not know, with the result that they libeled the God Whom they professed to extol, and degraded the national conception of God by misrepresentations, enforcing a righteousness which was external, exclusive, and evasive.

The result was the degradation of all life; the degradation of their own spirit to the hard, harsh, critical, cynical, self-satisfied temper which they manifested, the degradation of all their disciples, on whom they laid burdens that they themselves would not lift.

As Jesus moved among these men, the most religious and the most orthodox of men, He flung himself with holy passion and fervor, and strangely biting words of sarcastic denunciation against their righteousness, against the conception of righteousness, against their attempt to establish righteousness. I will defy you to find me a single unkind or harsh word Jesus ever spoke to sinning man or woman; harsh words were all reserved for false religious teachers, men who misinterpreted God to other men, and who cut the nerve of essential righteousness by attempting to substitute for it the righteousness of triviality and tradition, men who did not know God. Against these he hurled the final anathemas, the awful, appalling woes, of the 23rd chapter of Matthew (Morgan, pp. 305-310).

As Morgan points out, the Pharisees emerged in the mid-second century before Christ and they saved Judaism and the nation from being absorbed by Greek culture. This proves once again that God was not "silent" or on vacation during the centuries between Malachi and the time of Christ. God was working in the midst of His people and kept His promise to protect and preserve them as a nation. His deliverance through the flawed Maccabean leaders was something the Jews celebrated and commemorated and do to this day during the Hannukah holiday.

A knowledge of this historical foundation simply added to their confusion about Jesus' kingdom of God message, for the Jews and especially the Pharisees were looking for someone who would be a deliverer king like David and a meticulous Law-keeper like Moses. They were convinced that they were the chosen people and that God would not choose anyone else unless they first (or later as the Judaizers who tormented Paul) came into a relationship with the God of the Torah.

As Father Michael wrote earlier, the centuries before Jesus came are often referred to as the silent years, but in his and my estimation, they were anything but silent. Let's continue to examine why we have come to that conclusion in the next chapter.

Chapter 11

The So-Called Silent Years

John Stanko

Was God asleep or on vacation during the four centuries before Jesus was born? Did He become incommunicado with His people? That is hardly the case. God was at work not only revealing His love and fulfilling His covenant promises to His people but was also shaping the world in preparation for the Incarnation. Concerning those silent years, Charles Pfeiffer (1959) wrote,

> The time between the close of Old Testament history and the beginning of the New Testament has often been called "the 400 silent years." To the historian, however, these centuries were anything but silent, and they seem to become more vocal with each passing decade.
>
> To the student of ancient history, names like Cyrus, Darius, and Alexander the Great make this period one of paramount importance. The Jew notes during these centuries the development of synagogue worship, the successful Maccabean revolt, and the emergence of those parties within Judaism which have set the pattern for Jewish life and thought during the past two millennia.
>
> The Christian looks upon the Old Testament as preparatory, looking toward the fulfillment of its hopes and promises in the person of Jesus Christ. He is interested in the history of the centuries preceding the coming of Christ, for he sees them as a preparation for the advent, and a progress toward that period of history termed "the fullness of time" (Galatians 4:4).

The Dead Sea Scrolls have done much to quicken an interest in the literature of the Jews during the inter-Testament period. It is the purpose of this brief volume to outline the broader background necessary for the appraisal of these movements which immediately proceed the advent of the Savior (Pfeiffer, preface page).

Hellenism

Let's take a moment to do what Pfieffer mentioned above: outline a broader background of the years preceding Jesus' birth. The Maccabees and later the Pharisees were at war not so much with a people group or nation but with a philosophy or cultural trend. They were all resisting the effects of Hellenism and its real and perceived encroachment on Jewish life and culture. We can look back now and see what God was doing through this Greek influence:

1. He established a common language that would be used in communicating the truths and stories of the New Testament.

2. He paved the way for the Romans to take the place of Alexander the Great, thus providing a transportation and security network that would span much of the known world.

3. He broadened the narrow restrictions of Judaism that would pave the way for a Gentile influx of believers into the early church.

How can I make these claims about the role of Hellenism in New Testament times? Let's again turn to Charles Pfeiffer (1959) for the explanation:

At no time after the Babylonian exile did the majority of Jews live in Palestine. Many remained in their settlements in Babylon, or settled in other parts of the Tigris-Euphrates valley. Others went to Syria where there were large Jewish settlements, particularly in Antioch and Damascus. Asia Minor had large Jewish communities. Lydia, Phrygia, Ephesus, Pergamum, and Sardis all had numerous Jews in their population. The account of the visitors to Jerusalem on the day of Pentecost (Acts 2) and the journeys of the apostle Paul give us a significant picture of the settlements of the Jews of the Dispersion. These Jews remained loyal to the Jerusalem Temple. Every male Israelite over the age of 20 was expected to pay his Temple dues, and pilgrimages were made whenever possible. Each settlement, however, took on something of the characteristics of its neighbors, so that the Jews of Babylon would not have the same attitudes as those of Egypt. Those of Palestine would be apt to consider themselves alone the truly orthodox.

The most significant group of Jews of the Dispersion, historically speaking, was that of Alexandria. From the initial settlement of Alexandria the Jews had formed one of the most important and largest segments of the city where was the temptation to assimilate to the prevailing Hellenistic pattern, and here also was the determination to remain true to the faith.

Even for those who might not be tempted

by such a prospect of a life of ease, there were other aspects of Hellenism that seemed to offer a fuller life than the older ways. The merchant class was able to amass great wealth which could purchase better housing and food than the pre-Hellenistic world could have imagined. Great libraries in Alexandria and other Hellenistic centers, together with schools emphasizing a Greek education, would have appealed to many of the nobler youth of Israel. Sculpture and the fine arts offered an aesthetic outlook which would be frowned upon by the orthodox but which would make an impact on the young in particular. In Alexandria a synthesis developed between Judaism and Hellenism (pp. 84-85).

Since the Jews were spread out over the area of the Mediterranean and beyond and were subject to Hellenistic influence, the Greek language gave them some means through which to communicate their common ancestry and devotion to Judaism. Yet this language meant they could not read or discuss religious issues or concepts and necessitated a massive translation project of the Scriptures into Greek, which came to be known as the Septuagint which Father Michael talked about earlier.

Hellenism in Palestine

In the New Testament, we read this story about the early church:

In those days when the number of disciples was increasing, the Hellenistic Jews among them complained against the Hebraic Jews because their widows were being overlooked in the daily distribution of food. So the Twelve gathered all the disciples together and said, "It would not be right for us to neglect the ministry of the word of God in order to wait on tables. Brothers and sisters, choose seven men from among you who are known to be full of the Spirit and wisdom. We will turn this responsibility over to them and will give our attention to prayer and the ministry of the word."

This proposal pleased the whole group. They chose Stephen, a man full of faith and of the Holy Spirit; also Philip, Procorus, Nicanor, Timon, Parmenas, and Nicolas from Antioch, a convert to Judaism. They presented these men to the apostles, who prayed and laid their hands on them.

So the word of God spread. The number of disciples in Jerusalem increased rapidly, and a large number of priests became obedient to the faith (Acts 6:1-7, NIV).

What was the problem? Obviously, the church was growing and the leaders were scrambling to meet needs. Notice Luke was careful to tell us the identity of the people involved in the dispute: they were either Hellenists or Hebraic. The implication is that the group with the power, the local Jews from Jerusalem who were not prone to Hellenism (language and culture), were not disposed to helping those who, while also believers and Jews, considered to be Hellenistic. This makes clear the tension that existed between Jewish and Hellenistic cultures—and this was two hundred years after the Maccabees!

Charles Pfeiffer (1959) again provides the historical overview of Judaism and Hellenism:

Palestine itself was not so far removed from the centers of Hellenism as to be untouched. Especially the educated classes were enamored with the Greek way of doing things. The amphitheater and the gymnasium were attractive to the young, and a strong Hellenistic party emerged. In Judea, however, the lines were more closely drawn than they were in the dispersion. An anti-Hellenistic party arose which considered the Greek manner of life a threat to Judaism. The emphasis on things material, the nude appearance of the athletes in the gymnasium, the neglect of Jewish rites, were regarded as evidence of defection from the Law of God. The Hasidim, or the pious, were ready to defend their ancestral faith to the death if need be, and in the days of Antiochus Epiphanes, many of them did die for that faith. Future history shows us how necessary the Hasidim were in maintaining the place of the law of the Lord in a day of moral and spiritual decay. A generation that was tempted to accept the worst aspects of Hellenism life needed the corrective of a vibrant Hasidim (p. 90).

He further explained,

The rise of the Jewish sects is traceable to the impact of Hellenism on the life and culture of the near east. When the new clashes with the old, violent reactions frequently result. This is particularly true when the new ideology has religious and moral overtones.

Many of the Jews were willing to attempt a synthesis of Greek civilization and Hebrew religion. Jews in

Palestine as well as Jews throughout the Hellenistic world adopted Greek names, subscribed to Greek philosophy's, and looked to Greek institutions as the harbingers of cultural progress. The Jews in Palestine were generally more conservative than their Greek speaking cousins in Alexandria and the other great Hellenistic centers, but they were not unaffected. We may assume with these Jews felt that their loyalty to the faith of their fathers was in no way impaired by making peace with the new attitude which Alexander and his successors had advocated.

Other Jews reacted violently against the Hellenizers. They saw Hellenism as a way of life which was opposed to that prescribed in their Torah. The immodesty of the Greek gymnasium and the neglect of Jewish religious rites by the Hellenistically minded younger generation seemed to indicate trouble. As idolatry had been the besetting sin of Israel before the Exile, so Hellenism was regarded as the new temptation to unfaithfulness.

The Jews who reacted against Hellenism are known as the Hasidim (Chasidim) or Assidians. They were, by definition, the party of the "the pious." As the Sadducees of New Testament times continued the basic ideology of the earlier Hellenizers, so the Pharisees and the Essenes sought to preserve the basic tenets of the Hasidim. The law of God was basic in Hasidic thought. They were willing to suffer martyrdom rather than transgress its precepts. They supported the sons of Mattathias in the early days of the Maccabean revolt, but they left the Hasmoneans as soon as their religious liberties had been won from the Seleucids. Freedom to obey the law was to them an adequate goal, and political independence was quite unnecessary (pp. 111-112).

The Septuagint

It certainly makes sense that Greek-speaking Jews scattered outside Palestine would desire to read and study their holy writings and it makes equal sense that their conservative Jewish brothers saw this as cause for concern or outright apostasy. This translation began a challenge that still exists today, and that is of how to take words and cultural concepts and interpret them in a way that will make sense to those in another culture using another language. As much as the translators would want to make it a word-for-word literal translation, it proved difficult then and still does today for the translation requires judgments and decisions of exactly how to produce an accurate translation. Pfeiffer (1959) writes,

> The greatest monument of Alexandria Judaism was, without question, the translation of the Hebrew Old Testament into the Greek vernacular. While the origin of this version is unknown, legend places the beginning of this translation in the reign of the first of the Ptolemies (Philadelphus). While the legends suggest that the work was done in order to provide a copy of the Hebrew Scriptures for the Alexandria library, it is more likely that the translation was made at the impulse of Alexandrian Jews who

wanted their Greek-speaking children to be able to read the Scriptures. As the mother tongue (Hebrew) was forgotten by the younger generation, some provision had to be made for the preservation of the Hebrew sacred literature in the popularly spoken Greek. The Torah, or Pentateuch, was translated sometime around 250 BC. The remainder of the canonical books of the Old Testament were subsequently translated, as were the Apocryphal books. By the time of Origen (third century AD) this entire collection was called "the Septuagint," although the term originally referred only to the Greek translation of the Pentateuch. That a copy found its way into the library need not be doubted (pp. 85-86).

Pfeiffer (1959) continued,

Although without question translated by Alexandrian Jews for their own use, the Septuagint did serve as a means of acquainting the non-Jew with the principles of Jewish faith and practice. No doubt a copy was placed in the famous Alexandrian library. When we come to New Testament times, we read of many "God fearers" among the Gentiles. In a real sense the Septuagint help to pave the way for the ministry of the apostle Paul and others who took the message of Christ to non-Jews as well as to Jews. The biblical preaching in the Greek-speaking world was based on the Septuagint text. Many of the New Testament quotations from the Old are taken from the Septuagint, although others are translated from the Hebrew and others do not accord perfectly with either the Hebrew or Greek texts which we know. In most if not all of these cases, the writers are apparently paraphrasing the Scripture which they assume to be known to the readers (p. 87).

So there you have the cultural components that shaped Judaism and the world when Jesus of Nazareth came on the scene announcing the arrival of God's Kingdom. And now you have another reason to read and perhaps even study the Apocrypha, for they provide more information to help us understand the worldview and mindset of the Jews in the first century AD.

What's more, we see that the political milieu was similar to what we know in the 21st century—one world super power, materialism, love for sports, the people of God's fascination and obsession with politics. All those things mitigated against the people hearing Jesus' Kingdom message then and still do now. We trust that as you read, your ability to navigate the cultural waters and currents in your day will be enhanced and that you will call God's people to repentance and holiness as you serve God in your generation.

Chapter 12

The Kingdom of God

John Stanko

If you are like me, you have perhaps wondered how Jesus' contemporaries could have gotten it so wrong where His mission and message were concerned. They saw miracles—the dead raised, the maimed healed, demons expelled who testified to Jesus' divinity while they were coming out—and heard His gracious words. How could they have not seen them as a confirmation of what He was saying? I have tried to provide some of the common thinking of Jesus' day in the previous chapters to explain why the Jews were so tone deaf to Jesus' Kingdom message.

When I was a young believer, I thought to myself, *If I had been there and had seen what they saw, I would have put my faith in Jesus*. That's a bold statement and I was confident of its truth. However, as I have grown older in the Lord, I no longer make that assumption. As I have matured, I have come to realize more about the dynamics that kept the people from seeing—besides the obvious one that God the Father had not revealed Jesus to the masses. Their problem was alluded to in Romans 12:1-2:

> Therefore, I urge you, brothers and sisters, in view of God's mercy, to offer your bodies as a living sacrifice, holy and pleasing to God—this is your true and proper worship. Do not conform to the pattern of this world, but be transformed by the renewing of your mind. Then you will be able to test and approve what God's will is—his good, pleasing and perfect will (NIV).

The problem was that much of Jesus' audience, especially the religious leaders and elite, had been conformed to their "world" and could not be transformed by the renewal of their minds. They had made many assumptions about who God was and how He would work to fulfill His promises, some of which were based on what God Himself had done in the past. Let me explain what I mean, but to do so, I must go back and retrace even more of Israel's history than I have presented so far. Let's start with the time of Daniel and as I paint with very broad strokes, I ask forgiveness in advance from those who may cringe at my cursory approach to try and explain so many centuries filled with much important history. Let's get started.

Let's go back to 587 BC when the nation of Judah was surrounded by the armies of Nebuchadnezzar, king of Babylon. The ten tribes to the north had been conquered and carried away into captivity 150 years before this but God had preserved Judah and Benjamin out of His great love for King David. However, God's patience ran out even for them in their obstinance and disobedience and Nebuchadnezzar conquered Jerusalem, destroyed the Temple, and carried its treasures of some of the city's residents off to Babylon, about 600 miles from their home.

Of course, this was quite a shock to the survivors. After all, they were God's people. He had promised His protection and had also made promises that they would rule the world with Him as the King, but there they were, serving a pagan ruler. The inconceivable had happened.

"In the third year of the reign of Jehoiakim King of Judah, Nebuchadnezzar King of Babylon came to Jerusalem and besieged it, and the Lord delivered Jehoiakim King of Judah, into his hands along with some of the articles from the temple of God, these, he carried off to the temple of his God in Babylonia and put in the treasure house of his God" (Daniel 1:1-2, NIV).

After roughly 70 years in captivity, some of the Jews were able to return to the area of Jerusalem, but the Temple was in ruins and the area subject to control of local tribes not favorably disposed toward the Jews. The people who returned had a heart to rebuild, which we read in the books of Ezra and Nehemiah that the people had some measure of success but not without their setbacks, and the latter state of the area was nothing compared to what it had been under David and Solomon.

Now let's fast forward a few centuries to the year 356, the significance of which is found in the birth of a man who came to be known as Alexander the Great. In his prime, Alexander conquered the known world from Egypt to India, attempting to unite his territory with one culture and language—Greek or what came to be known as Hellenism.

The problem was that Alexander died in 323 BC before he could firmly establish his rule over such a vast domain and his kingdom was divided among his generals, the two most significant of which were Seleucus and Ptolemy. Seleucus received the areas north of Judah that included the former conqueror Babylon while Ptolemy was awarded the region south of Judah to Egypt.

Since Judah was the bridge between the regions of these two empires, they were regularly conquered by one and then the other. If you read the historian Josephus' accounts of the history in the post-Alexander era, you read of great loss of life and repeated military campaigns with Judah as the target of conquest and oppression. Surely the remnant living there must have called upon the name of the Lord, reminding Him of His promises that one day, a descendant of David would rule and restore Israel to its former glory. They had to wonder when that day would come.

Not only was there political tension between Israel and its enemies, but there was also cultural tension. Remember I said that one of Alexander's goals was to establish a Greek culture throughout his empire that would include language, customs, education, and worship. This movement called Hellenism increasingly encroached on Israel and its ways, which were based on the Hebrew language, Scriptures, and Temple sacrifices with the synagogue as the center of Jewish daily life and weekly worship. Greek ways were still a problem for legalistic Jews in Jesus' day who were zealous to preserve the ways of the forefathers as we learned in the last chapter. More on that later.

The cultural and religious tension came to a head in the second century BC when one of the Seleucid kings had his fill of Jewish ways and determined to stamp out Jewish culture and customs and did so by focusing his attention on the rebuilt Temple. The king's name was Antiochus Epiphanes IV and his idea of transformation was to place his image in the Temple and to sacrifice a pig there. Of course, the Jewish residents were outraged and were led in revolt by one of Maccabean leaders, Judas Maccabeus (Maccabees is the Hebrew word for hammer).

In a stunning victory against steep odds, Judas was able to defeat the forces of Antiochus IV and cleanse the Temple, which all Jews commemorate every year at Hannukah. This victory was consistent with the Jewish belief that they were unique and special because Yahweh, their God, was with them. They also believed that military campaigns could play an important role in their future deliverance and rise to power as it had been during the time of David and the Maccabees. This attitude was of course prevalent during Jesus' lifetime.

The Maccabees proved to be better military

leaders than politicians. They assumed the role as king or governor, but found their people were a difficult group to lead for many reasons. It was during this time that the Pharisees, major opponents of Jesus' public ministry, came into existence as a voice crying out against the Hellenization of Jewish life. In a way, they were the equivalent of the Puritans in England centuries later who tried to preserve the "purity" of religious life from secular incursions.

About 100 years after the Maccabees came to power, the Romans became a world power and, as they did the rest of the world, brought Israel under their dominion somewhere around the middle of the first century. So once again, the Jews found themselves part of a larger political entity that was at war with their way of life. They had been the victims of countless wars and military campaigns for centuries that led them to believe it was only a matter of time before it would be their turn to "rule the roost" and be back on top.

This anticipation was obvious when John the Baptist came on the scene, for the people were on constant Messiah watch. Every day they were waiting for their deliverer to come, someone who would do like the Maccabees or David or some other leader from their past to conquer the heathen and establish God's kingdom.

The problem was that everyone had their own idea of how this was going to happen, but as a people, they hoped and waited. When they confronted John, they wanted to know one thing: "Are you the One we have been waiting for?" John had to disappoint them and say, "No, I am not the one." Then came Jesus and the first words out of His mouth were, "The kingdom of God has come near. Repent and believe the good news!" (Mark 1:15, NIV). And the people heard, "Finally, someone who knows what it's going to take to defeat the godless and enthrone the King of kings and Lord of lords. It's time for a new sheriff in town and we're it." In fact, we read that they were ready to install Him on a throne:

> After the people saw the sign Jesus performed, they began to say, "Surely this is the Prophet who is to come into the world." Jesus, knowing that they intended to come and make him king by force, withdrew again to a mountain by himself (John 6:14-15, NIV).

Notice that they concluded Jesus was the Prophet to come, which they equated with their king after the order of King David.

Yet Jesus introduced a radical new concept of God's kingdom when He not only told them that God's kingdom was not of this world, but also that God was ready to let Israel's enemies "off the hook" so to speak through the practice of love and forgiveness:

> "You have heard that it was said, 'Love your neighbor and hate your enemy.' But I tell you, love your enemies and pray for those who persecute you, that you may be children of your Father in heaven. He causes his sun to rise on the evil and the good and sends rain on the righteous and the unrighteous. If you love those who love you, what reward will you get? Are not even the tax collectors doing that? And if you greet only your own people, what are you doing more than others? Do not even pagans do that? Be perfect, therefore, as your heavenly Father is perfect" (Matthew 5:43-48, NIV).

> Jesus said, "My kingdom is not of this world. If it were, my servants would fight to prevent my arrest by the Jewish

leaders. But now my kingdom is from another place" (John 18:36, NIV).

Jesus didn't say that what he was doing wouldn't impact the world, but His focus was not on establishing an earthly kingdom, but a spiritual kingdom. That's the essence of the gospel message and first-century Jewish ears were not ready to hear such talk. It's easy to understand why the "sinners" grasped His message long before most of the religious leaders did, for the latter were looking for something completely different.

My point in sharing all this is to point out that the books I am calling Apocryphal and Father Michael is referring to as Deuterocanonical give us the background we need to understand why the people were so eager for a military Messiah, hoping either John or Jesus was the One, but then so disappointed when they were not—or at least were not according to popular expectation.

The stories in the Apocrypha reinforced Israel's hope of God's intervention in human history to raise up a people for His own sake. These books showed that God had continued to be present in the lives of the nation right up to Jesus' birth. They told the people that God would deliver them not necessarily through superior numbers but through His direct intervention. The books had fed and fanned the flames of Jewish nationalism that were burning with great intensity when Jesus began His public ministry.

What's more, we learn from the Apocrypha that the people of Jesus' day were as politicized as our current generation. They were looking for a political solution to their spiritual problems and the nation was divided as to how that would take place. Consider the fact that when Jesus launched His public ministry there were Herodians (we didn't even discuss his rise to power as the puppet king of Rome over the Jewish people) who were probably loyal to Rome as the rulers of Israel; the Sadducees who ruled the Temple as appointees of Rome; the Pharisees, those who advocated for continued separation from the ways of the world; the Hellenists who did not oppose Greek influences in Jewish life to varying degrees; the Zealots who wanted to defeat the Romans through violence, and the people who also had a variety of their own ideas of what the Messiah was going to look like and do when He finally arrived.

Thus, when Jesus used the word "kingdom," every one of those groups had an idea of what they thought He meant and each one felt their way was the right. After all, even Jesus' closest disciples kept asking Him when He was going to restore the Kingdom right up to the time of His Ascension: "Then they gathered around him and asked him, "Lord, are you at this time going to restore the kingdom to Israel?" (Acts 1:6, NIV). Before then, we read of the disappointment of the disciples who were on the road to Emmaus when they said in Luke 24:20-21, "The chief priests and our rulers handed him over to be sentenced to death, and they crucified him; but we had hoped that he was the one who was going to redeem Israel" (NIV).

Since everyone had such a deeply ingrained idea of what the Kingdom was going to look like, it makes more sense that they could not comprehend Jesus' mission, even when His message was accompanied by signs and wonders. How could a "man" who did so much good but who had such a confused idea of Jewish supremacy that was rooted in the will of God be the One they were waiting for? Depending on what groupthink position I subscribed to and with which I agreed would have determined if I would have believed Jesus when I had beheld what He did. Even signs and wonders would not have convinced me to change my thinking on the Messiah and His role in God's Kingdom, once my mind was made up.

I attempted this brief and simplistic overview to give you a historic context for why the Apocrypha is so important for us today. They help us understand the context for the gospel accounts and give us an idea of the mindset Jesus was confronting. It also gives us an idea of what we face in the modern Church as we proclaim the Gospel to an audience made up of people who have their own interpretations of what the Church should or should not be.

Now let's hear from Father Michael again before I return to conclude our presentation on this subject matter.

Concluding Reflection

As I (Michael) reflect on the completion of this book—I am grateful for the open mindedness of Dr. John for even considering such a project. As a theologian and as one very interested in the history of the Church, I am deeply grieved that these important books (affectionately known as the Deuterocanonical books) are not only ignored, but are also neglected by many of those who nevertheless believe that God has continually intervened in history. The psalmist was clear that God is indignant on a daily basis (see Psalm 7:11). God is a God who is always involved in the lives of His people.

I trust that this short introduction will provide the scholar and casual reader with a hunger for a broader understanding of the biblical landscape that formed the New Testament world. I have tried to explain the Deuterocanonical books by showing a continuity that reflects their union with those books that have been accepted (since the Reformation) by most of the Christian world.

If you are accustomed to reading ancient commentaries, you will see these books cited along with other Scriptures with no distinction in authority considered. I have tried to give an honest record of the history of the development of the Canon of Scripture (which most believers that I have engaged with unfortunately are unfamiliar with, an ignorance that we must address). The African Code of 419 AD provides us with an authoritative statement that these 72/73 books could only be read in Church. The list was then sent to Rome for ratification. The Eastern Orthodox Church also holds to this same tradition as regards the Canon of Scripture with very little variation.

There are other Apocryphal (hidden) books that were never sanctioned by the bishops that are spurious (e.g. the Gospel of Thomas) and should not be trusted as valid. This, however, is not the case with the Deuterocanonical books that have always been considered to be sacred Scripture. Before I close, let me include something from St. Augustine in which he discussed what he considered to be the books of the Bible:

> Now the whole canon of Scripture on which we say this judgment is to be exercised, is contained in the following books: Five books of Moses, that is, Genesis, Exodus, Leviticus, Numbers, Deuteronomy; one book of Joshua the son of Nun; one of Judges; one short book called Ruth, which seems rather to belong to the beginning of Kings; next, four books of Kings [equal to 1 and 2 Samuel and 1 and 2 Kings], and two of Chronicles—these last not following one another, but running parallel, so to speak, and going over the same ground. The books now mentioned are history, which contains a connected narrative of the times, and follows the order of the events.
>
> There are other books which seem to follow no regular order, and are connected neither with the order of the preceding books nor with one another, such as Job, and Tobias, and Esther, and Judith, and the two books of Maccabees, and the two of Ezra, which last look more like a sequel to the continuous regular

history which terminates with the books of Kings and Chronicles.

Next are the Prophets, in which there is one book of the Psalms of David; and three books of Solomon, viz., Proverbs, Song of Songs, and Ecclesiastes. For two books, one called Wisdom and the other Ecclesiasticus, are ascribed to Solomon from a certain resemblance of style, but the most likely opinion is that they were written by Jesus the son of Sirach. Still they are to be reckoned among the prophetical books, since they have attained recognition as being authoritative.

The remainder are the books which are strictly called the Prophets: twelve separate books of the prophets which are connected with one another, and having never been disjoined, are reckoned as one book; the names of these prophets are as follows: Hosea, Joel, Amos, Obadiah, Jonah, Micah, Nahum, Habakkuk, Zephaniah, Haggai, Zechariah, Malachi; then there are the four greater prophets, Isaiah, Jeremiah, Daniel, Ezekiel. The authority of the Old Testament is contained within the limits of these forty-four books (Augustine, *On Christian Doctrine*, 2:8).

Thank you for considering the content of this book—may God richly bless you with insight. Beware that there are many versions of the "truth" in this subject area and many discussions are emotionally charged because of underlying biases. Please be open-minded—however, it eventually comes down to something the great G.K. Chesterton declared, "It shows that you value nothing if you don't make a decision!" The choice is yours after you examine the evidence objectively, hopefully with no prejudice because of emotion or church affiliation as to the validity and place of the Deuterocanonical books. Please stick to the facts, which will take further research but the end result will be as Scripture declares—"but you will know the truth and the truth shall set you free" (St. John 8:32).

Another Concluding Reflection

Now I (John) want to thank Father Pacella for his patience and diligence in getting this book project completed. In the process, Father Michael would send me pictures of book pages he was reading and web links and preached messages by various scholars that pertained to the subject matter of this book. It was a learning experience for me (one is never around Father Michael and not learning due to his commitment to scholarship and intellectual growth), and I have to say I have noticed many more Apocryphal references in my own reading that I'm sure I would have passed over if it had not been for this book. Thanks, Father Michael, for expanding my world once again through your love for church history and the traditions of the Church.

In my book titled *Pandemic Proverbs*, which was a summary of all my social media posts during the pandemic, I actually used a verse from my Apocryphal readings: "Do not keep your hand open to receive and close it when it is your turn to give" (Ecclesiasticus 4:31). A pastor friend used this verse in a preached message but mistakenly assumed it was from Ecclesiastes, since this pastor was not familiar with Ecclesiasticus. When some congregants brought this to the pastor's attention, they called me to ask if I had made a mistake. We had a good laugh over it, but I thought of what Father Michael had written earlier in this book.

Our unfamiliarity with the Apocryphal, dare I say Deuterocanonical books, needs to be corrected, for if there is content there that can build up and edify the saints, then I for one am all for it.

May the Lord bless the reading of His word and may we all be open to His revelation and illumination no matter how He chooses to give them to us.

References

Ellis, E. Earle. *Paul's Use of the Old Testament*. (Eugene, OR: Wipf and Stock Publishers, 1981).

Goodspeed, Edgar J. (translator). *The Apocrypha*. (New York: Vintage Books, a division of Random House, 1959).

Hahn, Scott W. *The Catholic Dictionary* (New York: Random House, 2009).

Morgan, G. Campbell. *The Westminster Pulpit, Volume VI: The Preaching of G. Campbell Morgan*. (Grand Rapids: Baker House 1954-1955).

Pfeiffer, Charles. *Between the Testaments*. Grand Rapids: Baker Book House,1959).

Saint Augustine, *On Christian Doctrine* (Radford, VA: Wilder Publications, 2013).

Wright, N. T., and Bird, Michael F. *The New Testament in Its World*. (Grand Rapids: Zondervan Academic, 2019).

How To Get In Touch With the Authors

Father Michael Pacella can be reached at

saintmichaelschurch14@gmail.com

Father Pacella's book, *From Valor to Virtue: The Moral Development of the Brave*, is available on Amazon in paper and Kindle formats.

*****

Dr. John Stanko is available at
johnstanko@gmail.com or any of his blog sites:

www.purposequest.com
www.johnstanko.us
www.stankobiblestudy.com
www.stankomondaymemo.com

All Dr. Stanko's books are available on Amazon.

For information on how to publish through Urban Press, contact Dr. Stanko at johnstanko@purposequest.com.

www.ingramcontent.com/pod-product-compliance
Lightning Source LLC
Chambersburg PA
CBHW060007050426
42447CB00027B/1745